HOW DOES THE ONE WHO SEEKS AFTER GOD PRODUCE RESULTS?

The first step is to contact the power that can change lives and heal.

The second is to turn that power on.

The third is to believe that this power is actually being transmitted through us and to accept it by faith.

AGNES SANFORD
THE HEALING LIGHT

Other BALLANTINE/EPIPHANY titles

AGNES SANFORD

THE HEALING LIGHT

BALLANTINE BOOKS • NEW YORK

DEDICATED
to
My Husband
Edgar Lewis Sanford

CONTENTS

CONTENTS

ORIGINAL INTRODUCTION

"The scientific attitude is the attitude of perfect open-mindedness," writes Agnes Sanford. *"It consists in an unshakable faith in the laws of nature combined with perfect humility toward those laws and a patient determination to learn them at whatever cost. Through this humility scientists have learned how to conform to the laws of nature and by so doing have achieved results. Through the same meekness those who seek God can produce results by learning to conform to His laws of faith and love.*

"The first step in seeking to produce results by any power is to contact that power. . . .

"The second step is to turn it on. . . .

"The third step is to believe that this power is coming into use and to accept it by faith. No matter how much we ask for something it becomes ours only as we accept it and give thanks for it."

These three steps are made so clear in this book that a child can understand them. But *something besides* understanding is required if one desires real healing and that "something besides" is what this book proceeds to give.

That "something besides" which Agnes Sanford possesses more than anyone I have met is hard to catch and put into words; it is something as evanescent and indefinable as the air we breathe. For want of a better word I shall call it the "climate" necessary for healing.

In Northern Siberia there is a Russian port, used for whaling vessels in the summer season. But in winter with the temperatures ranging from fifty to ninety degrees below zero, no vessels have ever been known to enter. The port is there, the wharves are there, all the avenues for ships to come and go are there. But no vessels ever come. It would be silly to ask why because everyone knows why they don't come in. It is because of the wrong kind of climate.

Anyone who steps into the presence of Agnes steps into the right kind of climate for healing. When I looked over the manuscript of this book I had only a secondary interest in seeing whether she had the "technique" of healing because I knew she had that. I knew that thousands of people who have never healed anyone in their lives also have the technique. My primary interest was in seeing whether this book (prepared for a world where the spiritual temperature is so far below zero) could furnish a "climate" that would make healing a living reality. To my great joy I found that this is exactly what it does do. I therefore put it on my MUST list for all who wish to go "all out" in their seeking for the healing power of God.

Agnes Sanford was born in China as the daughter of a Presbyterian missionary, she has lived for years in New Jersey as the wife of an Episcopalian rector, and she has studied and tried every form of healing that has ever been known. Never have I met one who combined the metaphysical and the sacramental approach as she does. I have never met anyone more Christ-centered nor anyone more church-centered and yet more utterly unconcerned about the creed or lack of creed of those that she administers to.

"I explained to the suffering soldier boy that there was a

healing energy in him that the doctors called 'nature,' that this same healing life was in the world outside of him too, and that he could receive more of it by asking for it.

'' 'Who'll I ask?' Sammy wondered.

'' 'Ask God. Because He is the one who made nature and He's in nature and He is nature.'

'' 'But I don't know anything about God.'

'' 'You know there's *something* outside of yourself, don't you? After all, you didn't make this world. There's *some* kind of life outside of you.'

'' 'Oh, sure. When you're scared enough you feel like there must be something.'

'' 'Well then, ask that Something to come into you. Just say ''Whoever you are or whatever you are, come into me now and help nature in my body to mend this bone.'' ' ''

This book shows how this boy and scores of others like him were healed through simple exposure to the climate of faith and love. If to this faith and love there is added the warm sunshine of enthusiasm, humor and good cheer there is nothing more to be asked. When you finish reading this book you will agree with me that this is far more than a book on healing. It is a guide to redemptive, creative living.

GLENN CLARK

St. Paul, Minnesota
1947

FOREWORD TO
REVISED EDITION

Many people have told me that there is a healing quality in
this book. As my editor, David Manuel, Jr., expressed it:

"*The Healing Light* is truly a remarkable book, filled
with love and light and an indefinable charismatic power
which has stood the test of more than a quarter-century.
The Lord will use it as a .channel for a great many more
healings—spiritual and mental, as much as physical—in a
whole new generation of Christians, for it is a faith-builder
of the first order. One reads it and gradually knows that
God will answer paryers for healing."

This must be true. Recently I read through this book,
written thrity years ago, in order to check it for this new
printing. In reading it I too received a healing. After a day
of immersion in it I felt ten years younger!

Perhaps this is because *The Healing Light* records my
very first steps into the new world wherein Jesus Christ
lives and moves in the soul of man, and through His
indwelling Spirit heals mind and body. Since then I have
of course known other spiritual experiences, but none any
greater than this first simple discovery that Jesus Christ is
here with us and heals today. Indeed, this basic experience

of the life of Jesus in us, healing and strengthening, is the best foundation for all other spiritual adventures.

In a way this is a do-it-yourself book, for its theme is that we ourselves can learn to open the door to our Lord so that He can come in and re-make our lives. We do not need to wait in the vain hope that some day He will get a big battering-ram and break down that door.

For many months the original manuscript of *The Healing Light* traveled about seeking a publisher. For another year or so it lay disconsolately in a bureau drawer, having found no one who would dare to believe it. At last it was discovered and published by Macalester Park Publishing Company, and it is still published by them and also by Arthur James, Publisher, in England. The hardback edition having sold continuously over the years, I am grateful that arrangements have now been made permitting its publication in a pocket edition as well.

May the Lord go with *The Healing Light* wherever it goes, and may He move in the heart of everyone who reads it!

Monrovia,   Agnes Sanford,
California   February, 1972

1

God Works
Through Us

If we try turning on an electric iron and it does not work,
we look to the wiring of the iron, the cord, or the house.
We do not stand in dismay before the iron and cry, "Oh,
electricity, *please* come into my iron and make it work!"
We realize that while the whole world is full of that
mysterious power we call electricity, only the amount that
flows through the wiring of the iron will make the iron
work for us.

The same principle is true of the creative energy of God.
The whole universe is full of it, but only the amount of it
that flows through our own beings will work for us.

We have tried often to make this creative power flow
through us, saying, "Oh, God, please do this or that!"
And He has not done this or that, so we have concluded
that there is no use in prayer, because God, if there is such
a Being, will do as He likes regardless of our wishes. In
other words, we doubt the *willingness* or the *ability* of God
to actually produce within our lives and bodies the results
that we desire. We do not doubt our own ability to come
into His presence and fill ourselves with Him, but His
willingness to come into us and fill us with Himself.

1

My baby had been ill for six weeks with abscessed ears. I prayed desperately that God would heal the child. My mind was filled with thoughts of fear and of bitterness, and these are not of God. God is love, and perfect love casts out fear. So God could not go through me to heal my baby, for there was a break in the pipeline that connected me with Him.

Nevertheless, in His great kindness He did what He could for me. He sent me one of His own ministers. The minister was a young man, ruddy-faced, clear-eyed, full of normal, healthy interest in people and in life.

"I'll go up and have a prayer with him," he said.

"I don't think that will do any good," I replied wearily. "He's only a year and a half old. He wouldn't understand."

What I really thought was, "If God doesn't answer *my* prayers, why would He answer this minister's prayers?"

"Oh, that won't matter," cried the minister, disregarding my feeble protests. He went upstairs.

Light shone in his eyes. I looked at him and saw his joyfulness, and I believed. For joy is the heavenly "O.K." on the inner life of power. No dreary, long-faced minister could have channeled God's healing to my baby, and it was the joy on the minister's face that called forth my faith. Looking on him I knew that he had been with the One who came to give us His joy, and so I knew that the baby would be well.

The minister placed his hands upon the baby's ears and said, "Now you close your eyes and go to sleep. I'm going to ask God to come into your ears and make them well, and when you wake up you'll be all right."

He did ask God exactly that, in the simplest possible way. He closed his prayer by saying, "We thank you, Heavenly Father, because we know that this is being done. Amen."

The fever-flush died out of the baby's face immediately. He turned very pale, closed his eyes and slept. When he woke, he was well. And he never again has had abscessed ears.

This incident turned on the light for me in the world that had grown very dark with futility. It showed me that God is an *active* and *powerful* reality. True, I understood very little about Him. I merely thought that the visiting minister had the gift of healing. Now I know that he had no gift except that which is open to all of us, the infinite gift of the life of God Himself. God's water of life could rush through him, for the pipeline between his spirit and God's spirit was intact. He was in harmony with God. The life of God flowed through him, and could therefore be turned on by him for the healing of a child. He *knew* it, and therefore had the courage to speak with authority.

"We thank you because we know that this is being done," he had said, adding the word, "Amen (So be it)," a word of command. All prayers end with "Amen," but usually the word is meaningless. The people who utter it do not in the least intend to send forth a command so positive that they would dare to say, "When he wakes he will be all right." This is one reason many prayers do not seem to be answered.

God is both within us and without us. He is the source of all life; the creator of universe behind universe; and of unimaginable depths of inter-stellar space and of light-years without end. But He is also the indwelling life of our own little selves. And just as a whole world full of electricity will not light a house unless the house itself is prepared to receive that electricity, so the infinite and eternal life of God cannot help us unless we are prepared to receive that life within ourselves. *Only the amount of God that we can get in us will work for us*.

"The kingdom of God is within you," said Jesus. And it is the indwelling light, the secret place of the consciousness of the Most High that is the kingdom of Heaven in its present manifestation on this earth. Learning to live in the kingdom of Heaven is learning to turn on the light of God within.

We must learn that God is not an unreasonable and impulsive sovereign who breaks His own laws at will. As soon as we learn that God does things *through* us (not *for* us), the matter becomes as simple as breathing, as inevitable as sunrise.

"But God is omnipotent!" some people say. "He can do anything He likes!" Certainly, but He has made a world that runs by law, and He does not like to break those laws.

Few of us in the north would ask God to produce a full-blown rose out of doors in January. Yet He can do this very thing, if we adapt our greenhouses to His laws of heat and light, so as to provide the necessities of the rose. And He can produce a full-blown answer to prayer if we adapt our earthly tabernacles to His laws of love and faith so as to provide the necessities of answered prayer.

Some day the world will come to understand this fact, as it is now beginning to understand the miracle of light waves, for one generation's miracles are the commonplaces of another generation.

Some day we will understand the principles that underlie the miracle-working powers of God, and we will accept His intervention as simply and naturally as we do the radio and television that cause us to see and hear a person far away both in space and in time.

But that was not a breaking of the laws of nature. It was the super-imposition of a higher law of life over a lower law of life. Thus it was the fulfillment of the laws of nature. If one thinks of a miracle not as the breaking of God's laws but as His own using of His laws, then the world is full of miracles.

I have seen pneumonia destroyed within fifteen minutes, while the patient's temperature dropped from a hundred-and-three to normal and perspiration poured from his body and drenched the sheets. This was almost as great a miracle as the miracle of the frost, weaving ever-changing patterns on the window-pane. It was almost as great a miracle as the miracle of day and night, of sunrise and sunset, caused by the never-ceasing swing of the earth and the sun and the moon in a pattern of motion controlled and adjusted by cosmic forces beyond the ken of the astronomer.

God does nothing except by law. But He has provided enough power within His laws to do anything that is in accordance with His will. His will includes unlimited miracles. It is for us to learn His will, to seek the simplicity and the beauty of the laws that set free His power.

2

Experiments
In Prayer

The One who knew said, "Blessed are the poor in spirit, for theirs is the Kingdom of Heaven." Happy, that is, are those people who know that their spiritual power is small, that their creeds are imperfect, that their instruction concerning God and man is incomplete. Happy are those who know that they do not know all of truth. For only those who admit their spiritual poverty are willing to learn.

One way to understand a hitherto unexplored force of nature is to experiment with that force intelligently and with an open mind. This book suggests, for those willing to learn, a method so simple that it is childlike, as the more profound truths are apt to be. It is an experimental method. One decides upon a definite subject for prayer, prays about it and then decides whether or not the prayer-project succeeds. If it does not succeed, one seeks a better adjustment with God and tries again.

"Blessed are the meek, for they shall inherit the earth." The attitude of perfect meekness consists of an unshakable faith in the laws of nature combined with perfect humility toward those laws and a patient determination to learn them at whatever cost. Through this meekness we have learned how to conform to the laws of nature, and by so doing have achieved great results. Through the same meekness those who seek God can produce results by learning to conform to His laws of faith and love.

The first step in seeking to produce results by any power is to contact that power. The first step then in seeking help from God is to contact God. "Be still and know that I am God."

Let us then lay aside our worries and cares, quiet our minds and concentrate upon the reality of God. We may not know who God is or what God is, but we know that there is something that sustains this universe, and that something is not ourselves. So the first step is to relax and to remind ourselves that there is a source of life outside of ourselves.

The second step is to connect with this life by some such prayer as this: "Heavenly Father, please increase in me at this time your life-giving power."

The third step is to believe that this power is coming into use and to accept it by faith. No matter how much we ask for something it becomes ours only as we accept it and give thanks for it. "Thank you," we can say, "that your life is *now* coming into me and increasing life in my spirit and in my mind and in my body."

And the fourth step is to observe the operations of that light and life. In order to do so, we must decide on some tangible thing that we wish accomplished by that power, so that we can know without question whether our experiment succeeded or failed.

Many Christians are afraid to do this. A working woman once told me that she asked God to send her two pairs of rubbers for her sons, to protect their feet from rain and slush. That night, she said, the ground froze over solid and for two days the boys walked to school dry-shod. Upon the third day a neighbor gave her two pairs of rubbers for her sons.

"Oh, but I would never *dare* do that!" cried a young man to whom I repeated this. "Because—what if the rubbers didn't come?"

If the rubbers weren't forthcoming, he implied—there was no God. But if he had turned on an electric light and it had failed to shine, he would not have said, "There is no electricity!" He would have said, "There is something wrong with this lamp."

Let us understand then that if our experiment fails, it is not due to a lack in God, but to a natural and understandable lack in ourselves. What scientist would be discouraged if his first experiment failed? Since we intend with His help to heal our short-comings, to repair our wiring, we need not fear to test His power by prayer.

A pair of rubbers might not be the simplest objective, nor a new coat, nor a larger home. We might be mistaken concerning our need of these things. Moreover, the attaining of such things in prayer involves the swaying of more minds than ours, and is rather difficult for a first experiment. Let us choose one of the very simplest of prayer-experiments, remembering always that it must be tangible; that is, it must be something that we can put the finger on and say either "This has been done," or "This has not been done."

How strange it is that people who fear to do this do not hesitate to pray for the most difficult objectives of all, such as the peace of the world or the salvation of their souls! If they have so little confidence in prayer that they do not dare to test their powers of contacting God by praying for an easy thing, it is probable that their cosmic intercessions are of little force. If everyone who prayed for the peace of the world had enough prayer-power to accomplish the healing of a head cold, this would be a different world within twenty-four hours.

All the cattle on a thousand hills are His, all the rubbers in all the world are under His control, and sufficient power to heal the head colds of all humanity flows at His command. Let us not be afraid then, to choose for our first prayer-experiment an objective that is simple and personal. This objective must of course be in accordance with God's will, for it is as difficult to make God's power operate contrary to His will as it is to make water flow uphill. A wise engineer studies the laws of flowing water and builds his water system in accordance with those laws. A wise scientist studies the laws of nature and adapts his experiments to those laws. And a wise seeker after God had better study the laws of God and adapt his prayers to those laws.

There is no great mystery concerning the will of God, in so far as it applies to our small selves. God's will is written into His nature, and the nature of God is love. Therefore, when we pray in accordance with the law of love, we are praying in accordance with the will of God.

The simplest and most direct of all prayer-projects is the healing of the body. The body is indeed a laboratory exquisitely adapted to the working out of the power of God. And healing by some form of prayer or faith is as natural and as instinctive as breathing. It has been practiced, with or without understanding, by people of every age. It is as old as history and as modern as space travel. Almost everyone in times of great stress cries out to someone—to something—even if he does so only by a blind, instinctive urge and denies his own impulse immediately afterwards.

Much of this clamoring to deity has failed to produce results. Therefore a great many Christians, unwilling to believe that God cannot heal them, have persuaded themselves that He will not. In so doing they forget both the example and the words of Jesus Christ. He told us that God is a loving Father who delights to give good gifts to His children. But those parents and teachers who dimmed the shining of His eternal glory in our infant minds taught us that God often willed us to suffer. ''Well, God's will be done," they sighed, when prayer for health brought no relief from pain.

If we think of God as a heavenly stage manager, jerking us about like puppets upon strings, this is a natural and indeed an inevitable conclusion. God can do whatever He likes. We have asked him to make us well. He has not done so. Well, then, He must like us to be sick. In which case, if we are logical, we will not only stop praying for health but also stop taking medicine, for who are we to go against God's will? We are not logical, thank God. An inner wisdom deeper than reason forces us to strive always after life. We continue taking medicine, even while we sigh, "God's will be done." We also continue to cry, "Oh, Lord, please—!" even though it is only the instinctive howl of an infant for its mother.

When we realize that God is not only transcendent, He is also immanent—that is, He is not only in the heaven and the heaven of heavens, but also in our own small minds and bodies—then this difficulty disappears. We see that the lack of success in healing is not due to God's will for us but to our failure to live near enough to God so that He can accomplish perfection in our spirits and bodies, He will do the next best thing and endeavor with divine patience to teach us through suffering. In this case we are receiving as much of His life-giving spirit as He can get through to us, but not the full flow necessary to life.

When our electric lights work partially or not at all, we know that the lack of power is not in the universal and infinite and eternal flow of electricity in the universe, but in the wiring that connects us with that flow. When Edison had tried some hundreds of times to find a wire that could transmit a continuous flow of electricity, and had failed some hundreds of times, he did not say, "It is not the will of electricity to shine continuously in my wire." He tried again. He believed that it *was* in the will, that is, in the nature, of electricity to produce this steady light. He concluded, therefore, that there was some adjustment to the laws of electricity that he had not yet made, and he determined to make that adjustment. For more than six thousand times he tried again. And he succeeded in making electricity shine continuously in a wire. That is faith.

In certain very difficult cases there are adjustments to the laws of God that cannot be made perfectly in this lifetime. Even so, we do well to strive continually toward life in our prayers, even as we strive continually toward life in our medical care. If it is too late for the perfect healing of our bodies in this life we will at least receive enough of His power to enlighten our spirits and to relieve our pain.

I was once asked to pray for a little boy with abscessed ears. The child improved for twenty-four hours, then relapsed. I prayed with him again and the same thing happened again, more than once. Each relapse was worse than the last and he was finally taken to a hospital and operated upon for mastoid. Even the cooperation of prayer and science did not save him. The poison began to eat into the bones of the head. He was on the verge of spinal meningitis.

Feeling sure that since Jesus never failed to heal a little boy brought to Him by faithful parents and so we should never fail, I sought more power in prayer. My methods were perhaps childlike. But through them I learned, as children learn. I went to see the little boy in the company of a minister, and again with two or three friends, hoping by just the right combination of minds to provide God with the right kind of a wire for the inflowing of His power. The boy's condition grew steadily worse, as indeed the little fellow expected. He had had a number of desperate illnesses in his nine-year span of life, and had developed an invalid consciousness, the greatest possible barrier to healing.

"Nothing can make me well!" he would sigh. "I'm

always sicker than anybody else!'' And he would console himself in his trouble by taking pride in his ability to exceed others in being sick.

I found him on a certain Good Friday half-conscious and nearly blind in a darkened room. At this point Satan entered me and I began to wonder whether it was God's will for him to die. Upon my knees I wrestled with this problem, knowing that if I were to accept God's will for a little child as blindness, agony and death, my experiments in healing were over. If I had accepted death, the child would have died. And the parents would have consoled themselves forever by thinking, ''God's will be done.'' But I cut myself away from this convenient excuse for failure as a ship going out to sea drops its shore-lines. I telephoned to an older and more experienced prayer-worker from a neighboring city.

''The parents are the barriers, dearie,'' she said. ''They're afraid. They must stop being afraid.''

''I know,'' I confessed. ''But I just haven't the nerve to tell them they mustn't be afraid!''

''Send them to me,'' directed my prayer-partner. ''I'll tell them.''

She told them, and the serene and joyful assurance in her eyes strengthened their faith. She then directed me to go to the little boy at a certain time and place my hands upon him.

''But don't try to do anything, dearie,'' she advised me. ''You've been trying too hard, and it's upset you. Just be still and know; He is God and His power is flowing into you through me.''

I followed her directions. The child was by this time unconscious. He did not rouse as I stood beside him in the dark, my hands on his brow. Yet I was so conscious of a heavenly presence with us that I returned home giving thanks.

The parents went to see the child on Easter Sunday

afternoon. They heard the little boy singing before they reached his room. As they entered the door, they were met by blazing sunlight shining full across his bed. He was sitting up in bed, cutting pictures from a magazine and singing "Three Blind Mice" at the top of his voice.

Moreover, he lost his invalid consciousness and learned to live in the kingdom of Heaven. He was home within a week, spent the summer swimming and fishing, and went through the following winter with no illness at all. The next summer he caught a cold and I went to see him again.

"Do you remember how I taught you to talk to germs?" I asked him. "Have you been doing it?"

"Yeah-man!" cried the little boy. "And it's O.K. I've got a fever now, but that's just the healing things in me doing what God and me told 'em to do and killing the germs. Tomorrow I'll be O.K. You'll see!"

On the morrow he *was* "O.K."

Which was God's will? This, or the premature death of a little boy?

In the middle ages, many a child died of smallpox because science had not yet discovered the smallpox vaccine. Yet the vaccine was here all the time awaiting discovery. And many a person dies because humanity has not discovered His healing power as it operates through the being of men. Yet that power is here, awaiting our adjustment to it.

Deciding once for all, then, that God is a loving Father who delights to give good gifts to His children, let us learn how to accept those gifts. Let us choose as a prayer-objective the healing of the body, because it is a simple and obvious need.

When we ask for the indwelling of God's Holy Spirit in the body, let us think of that part of the body that most needs His life. Let us imagine His light and life glowing there like a fire, shining there like a light. Then through the rest of the day let us continually give thanks that His life is at work within us accomplishing His perfect will and recreating us after His image and likeness, which is perfection. If we have sought God for a simple thing such as healing of a cold in the head, we may find that healing perfected in a few minutes. If we have sought Him for the rebuilding of bones or nerves or sinuses, the complete healing may take time and patience. It would be well to make a special prayer for it at least twice every day, preferably on awaking and just before going to sleep. In this prayer we can ask for a renewal of God's healing power, remembering always to give thanks for what He has done and is continuing to do.

How long should we continue praying for healing? Until the healing is accomplished. Sometimes a prayer once or twice a day is sufficient, but sometimes we need to "pray without ceasing," to keep ourselves open to the continuous inflow of God's power. We do this, not by saying over and over again, "Oh please, Lord," for that sounds as though we do not believe He is really working. It is much better to keep the power flowing by continually giving thanks for it. Every time we think of a condition within ourselves that needs healing we can say, "Thank you, Lord, that your power is making me well." And we can look ahead and see ourselves well and strong.

In praying for another person in a critical condition we may need at times to hold that one up in almost continuous prayer, saying, "Thank you, Lord, that your healing power is being increased in this person, working toward perfect health."

There are other times when all we need to do is to remind ourselves of our real being as children of God, and His power works so rapidly that one prayer really is enough.

There was a small boy who had a leaky heart. I had prayed for the healing of the heart, but with slight success. The heart was better, but was not well. This was most unusual, as the healing of a child's heart is one of the easiest of prayer-objectives for me, and until this time I had never needed to pray for it but once. It came to me therefore that I needed active cooperation from the little boy. So I questioned him concerning his knowledge of God.

"I know all about God," he replied serenely. "God is in this room, only you can't see Him 'cause He's 'visible. And Jesus is in this room, only you can't see Him 'cause He's 'visible."

"Yes. Isn't that funny?"

"Not to me, it isn't."

Thus I was reproved. Billy, I decided, knew about God with more profound simplicity than I did. His theology was quite sufficient for his seven years. It remained only for me to teach him how to make his knowledge of God work for the healing of his heart.

"How about playing a little pretend-game with me?" I said to the small friend of God. "Pretend you're a big guy going to high school and you're on the football squad. Shut your eyes and see yourself holding the ball and running ahead of all the other fellows. 'Look at that guy!' the other kids will say. 'Just look at him run! Boy, he's strong! I bet he's got a strong heart!' Then you say, 'Thank you, God, because that's the way it's going to be.' Will you play that game every night, right after you say your going-to-bed prayers?"

I left Billy grinning but non-committal.

A month later I returned. The mother had taken Billy to the doctor, as I had requested her to do. The doctor knew of his patient's experiments with faith and was delighted to pronounce the heart perfect.

"Have you been playing my pretend-game, Billy?" I asked the small seeker after truth.

The little boy's face lit up with a delighted grin. "Sure have!" he cried.

He had played the game. And upon playing it he had

found therein a profound reality. Thus he had wrestled with God as his partner against the powers of destruction and had prevailed. The will of God for him was not a leaky heart, but health.

3

Turning On The Light Of God's Creative Energy

St. Paul advised the new Christians in Ephesus to "walk as children of light": to live, that is, as if they were made of a living, moving energy like light. A few centuries ago we would have thought this just a fanciful idea. Now, thanks to the scientists, we know that it is really true. For scientists have discovered that the body is not hard, solid matter, but is made up of specks of energy. These bits of energy attract and repel each other with tiny explosions of light. So in a very real way the body is full of light.

The oldest of all stories about creation tells us that God created light before He created the sun and the earth.

"But this is impossible," cried wise men of long ago. "There could be no light before the sun was made."

It is not impossible at all. For nowadays we know that light is a form of energy and that all created things are made of energy. As St. Paul says, "Things that are seen were not made of things which appear," for this primal light vibrates at too high an intensity and too fine a wave length for the human eye to see. We can understand this, too. We know that we cannot see the light of X-ray. Yet we know that it is more powerful than sunlight.

17

God made, first of all, *light*. And the Spirit of God moved upon the face of the deep, so the historian tells us, doing his best to put into the words at his disposal truths that even our modern term "inter-stellar space" does not adequately express.

We are therefore made, not of solid and impenetrable matter, but of energy. The very chemicals contained in the body—the "dust of the earth"—live by the breath of God, by the primal energy, the original force that we call God. This being so, it is not strange at all that when we establish a closer connection with God in prayer, we should receive more abundant life—an increased flow of energy. The creative force that sustains us is increased within our bodies.

The vibration of God's light is so very real that even a child can feel it, and it was my work with children that showed me the action of an invisible but powerful light-vibration shining from the Father of lights.

I went to see a little girl who had been in a cast for five months following infantile paralysis. One day I placed my hands above the rigid knee in that instinctive laying-on of hands that every mother knows. (What mother has not soothed a crying baby with the laying-on of hands? And what lover of animals has never calmed a nervous pet with the same soothing touch?) And I asked that the light of God might shine through me into the small, stiff knee and make it well.

"Oh, take your hands away!" cried the little girl. "It's hot."

"That's God's power working in your knee, Sally," I replied. "It's like electricity working in your lamp. I guess it has to be hot, so as to make the knee come back to life. So you just stand it now for a few minutes, while I tell you about Peter Rabbit."

By the time the erring Peter had returned home without his shoes and his new red jacket and had been put to bed with castor oil, the pulsation of energy in my hands had died away.

"Now crawl out to the edge of the bed, Sally, and see if that leg will bend," I directed the child.

She pulled herself to the edge of the bed and sat up. And the leg that had been rigid, bent at an angle of forty-five degrees. Within two weeks she was walking.

"How do you turn on God's electricity in your hands?" she asked me at my next visit.

"I don't turn it on," I replied. "I just forget everything else and think about God and about Jesus who is God's Son and our friend. And I believe that God can turn on that light in me because Jesus said He could. He turns it on, and when He is through with it, He turns it off."

Sally and I both understood quite simply that God's life was a kind of light. We could not see this light. But she felt it as heat. And I perceived through my hands and arms the flow of the invisible force that caused the heat. We did not have the scientific background to explain these things. But the guiding intelligence who leads us on toward truth directed me toward a man who could explain it.

I visited the daughter of a scientist to pray for her healing. Later she explained to him the feeling of inward heat that followed our prayer.

"I believe that," said the scientist, "because my studies in the vibrations of sight and sound have shown me that such a thing must be."

"Why?" I asked. "Can you tell me in simple words so that I can understand it?"

"There are vibrations of light that the human eye cannot register," he explained, "because they vibrate at too high an intensity and too fine a wave length."

"Like the light of an X-ray machine?" I asked him.

"Yes."

"You speak of this as a vibration," I replied. "But your daughter felt it as a heat. Why was that?"

"She did not feel the actual energy that entered her. She perceived only the effect of the energy and it felt to her like heat. It was not the heat that healed her. The light that you see in an electric bulb is not electricity itself. Electricity is invisible. The light is only the result of the electricity acting upon the wire."

So it is with the healing light of God. It is registered in different ways in different people. Most of us grown people have become so dull in spiritual perception that we do not feel it at all, even though it works toward a healing. But children nearly always perceive it, either as heat or as a force that they cannot describe but often compare to electricity.

Once I was called to see a baby girl ill with pneumonia. I knelt beside her crib in silence, laid one hand upon the small, congested chest and slipped the other one beneath her back, and asked God to come into her. Soon the waxy frame of the baby was filled with a visible inrushing of new life. Even the hands and feet vibrated, as if an electric current were entering into her. A look of tension on the tiny face was smoothed away and she passed from a semi-conscious condition into a natural sleep. Two hours later her doctor came into the room. He stopped at the threshold, eyes staring, jaw dropped in surprise. For he had come to report his hospital arrangements for the child and he beheld his small patient, bright-eyed and cheerful, sitting up in bed.

"Mine doctor," said she, "can I have a cookie?"

"My God!" exclaimed the doctor, startled out of his bedside manner. "What's happened to her?"

He was quite right. It was his God who had intervened—that was what had happened to her.

The power that causes light to shine within the electric light bulb is part of the electric light. In fact, although that force itself cannot be seen, it is as much a part of the electric light as the wire and the glass that make its framework. The spiritual force that flows through us is the "breath of God" breathed into the "dust of the earth" of which our frames are made. It is the eternal Being dwelling for a moment in a home of flesh.

"Ye are the light of the world," said that amazing carpenter whose light still shines down through the centuries. This is literally true. We are the electric light bulbs through whom the light of God reaches the world. Thus we are "part God." This does not belittle God, any more than it belittles the sun to know that a square of sunlight on the floor is part of its infinite and eternal shining.

Knowing then that we are part of God, that His life within us is an active energy and that He works through the laws of our bodies, let us study to adjust and conform ourselves to those laws. When we do this with understanding and common-sense, we can speed up the natural healing forces of the body.

One does not need to be a saint or a scientist in order to do this. I once worked as a volunteer in an army hospital, and I found that the ordinary G.I. could learn to speed up the healing processes of the body if he wanted to do so.

"What's the matter, Sammy?" I once asked a boy in an orthopedic ward. "You look sort of down in the mouth this morning."

"Oh, I'm sick of this business. The darn leg isn't mending at all, and now they tell me they're going to do another bone graft."

"Well, what's wrong with that? I think it's wonderful, the things they can do with bone grafts."

"Oh yeah? Well, you wouldn't if you'd been in traction for six months. They're going to wait another month before they even do it. Then they're going to take another X-ray. Then they're going to stick in two inches of bone and that'll mean another eight weeks in a cast."

"They must hope that nature will do it without a bone graft, or else they wouldn't wait."

"Oh, sure," grumbled Sammy. "But they've been figuring that way for about six months now. And every time, nature lies down on the job and they do another bone graft and then the bone graft don't take."

"I could tell you a way of getting nature back on the job, if you'd like to hear it," said I.

"Oh, there isn't any way. It's just a matter of time."

"That's not right, Sammy. There is a way of hurrying nature up. I know, because I've done it and I've seen other people do it. Want me to tell you?"

"Sure."

So I explained to Sammy that there was a healing energy in him that the doctors called "nature," that this same healing life was in the world outside of him too, and that he could receive more of it by asking for it.

"Who'll I ask?" Sammy wondered.

"Ask God. Because He is the one who made nature, and He's in nature, and He is nature."

"But I don't know anything about God."

"You know there's *something* outside of yourself, don't you? After all, you didn't make this world. There's *some* kind of life outside of you."

"Oh, sure. When you're scared enough, you feel like there must be something."

"Well, then, ask that Something to come into you. Just say 'Whoever you are or whatever you are, come into me now and help nature in my body to mend this bone, and do it quick. Thanks, I believe you're doing it.' Then make a picture in your mind of the leg well. Shut your eyes and see it that way. See the bone all built in and the flesh strong and perfect around it. And play like you see a kind of light shining in it—a sort of a blue light, like one of these neon signs, shining and burning and flowing all up and down the leg."

"Why do I do that?"

"Because that's the way you make it happen. No matter

what you want to make, you first have to see it in your mind, don't you? Could you make a table if you didn't first see in your mind the kind of table you're going to make?"

"I get it."

"Good! Then after you see the leg well, give a pep talk to all the healing forces of your body. Say, 'Look here, I'm boss inside of me and what I say goes. Now get busy and mend that leg.' And then congratulate them and tell them they're doing a good job, because they won't work for you unless you encourage them. And after this, forget them and think of the life outside of you again, and say, 'Thank you, God. I believe it's going to be O.K.' "

"How often must I do this?"

"Once a day at least, three times a day if it doesn't get tiresome. And always at the same time every day, because then you get in the habit of thinking like that at that time and it helps a lot. And don't work too hard at it! Before you start doing anything, get comfortable and relax. And just play it like a game. You can think of lots of other ways to play it. Imagine yourself running and jumping over fences and all kinds of things."

Three weeks later the boy was still in traction, but there was a pleased smile on his face.

"Come night when everybody's asleep," he told me under cover of a very noisy radio, "I unfasten this darn thing and get my leg out. Turn on my side, too. And it doesn't hurt."

"Oh, you shouldn't do that!" I cried. "Didn't I tell you not to try anything until the doctor gave the word?"

"Well, but I do, though," replied Sammy calmly. "And it doesn't hurt, either."

The following week he was in a wheel chair. "They took an X-ray," he grinned, "and the next day they said I could get up."

A month or so later I met him in the recreation hall, walking with a cane.

"Do you still do what I told you to do?" I asked him.

"Yep," he replied, "and I can walk, too, with a brace."

"Then you'll soon walk without a brace," I told him.

"I know it," he grinned, and a light flashed from his eyes to mine.

I wondered, as I went on my way to the PX, how much he knew now about God. Certainly he knew something that made him very happy!

After replenishing my stock of potato chips I saw him again, walking across the PX—without his cane—and very carefully not seeing me, like a little boy showing off.

For those who, like Sammy, have not been introduced to God, I will sum up the prayer of faith:

1. *Choose the same time and the same place every day, make yourself comfortable and relax.*

2. *Remind yourself of the reality of a life outside yourself.*

3. *Ask that life to come in and increase life in your body.*

4. *Make a picture in your mind of your body well.* Think especially of the part of the body that most needs to be well. See it well and perfect and shining with God's light. And give thanks that this is being accomplished.

And for those who know God and have long practiced prayer I will add a few suggestions and meditations that have proved helpful to me and may prove helpful to them.

In order to receive God's life in the body, we must first be able to forget the body so that we can quiet the mind and concentrate the spiritual energies on God. Let us sit comfortably with the head at rest and the hands folded in the lap. Many people find it helpful to meditate with the feet raised, resting upon a footstool or even upon another chair. The spine may be relaxed and comfortable as one sits, but it must not be curved or cramped. The one who prays will discover the reason for this as he connects more

and more closely with the life of God. He will find that he
is filled with such fullness of life that his spine must be
free so that his chest can expand. He will notice as he
relaxes that even his breathing is altered, becoming slow,
thin and light as if to leave room for the Spirit of God
within. If we consider the body just enough to make it
comfortable so that it can relax, the spirit will direct its
care and provide its needs.

"So that it can relax." How simple that sounds, yet
how few are able to do it! Most of us have become the
servants of nerves, so that we adjust ourselves according to
their tensions. We must teach them to be our servants,
adjusting themselves to our demands for more or less
tension. This can be done by a simple process of re-education.

"Now the nerves of my feet and legs are getting heavy
and still—heavy and still," we think drowsily. "I couldn't
lift them if I wanted to—they're getting heavy and still—
heavy and still—"

Nerves are like children. They respond to suggestion
better than to command. In fact the subconscious mind that
controls the forces of the body has an almost wanton
disregard for command. "Relax!" we tell ourselves sternly,
and the nerves laugh at us and tighten up more than ever.
"Now you're relaxing," we congratulate them, and with a
pleased smile they relax.

So we speak gently and soothingly to the nerves all the
way up the body and in the head. And in the same quiet
way we bid our conscious minds be still. The control
center that we call the subconscious mind conveys that
order to the brain.

Of course all this preparation for prayer makes use of
the law of suggestion.

"Prayer is only auto-suggestion," some people say.

Those who really experiment with prayer know from its
results that it is far more than auto-suggestion. It is the

inner being that is part of God speaking to the framework of flesh.

Having quieted our nerves and minds by sitting in the most comfortable position and by relaxing, let us now open our spirits to receive the more abundant life of God. How easy this becomes when we realize that God is not a far-away sovereign, but is actually the medium in which we live—the very breath of life! This is so, whether we know it or not. But the more we realize it, the more real it becomes to us. For as we tune in our thought-vibrations to the thought-vibrations of God we expose ourselves, as it were, to His eternal shining and so receive His image upon ourselves.

We receive God, in other words, by forgetting ourselves and thinking about Him. Therefore we begin our prayer, not by clamoring for this and that before we have even reached His presence, but by thinking about Him in the way that makes Him most real to us.

"Hallowed be Thy name." Thus begins the model prayer of all ages.

This is the most practical of all possible beginnings, because thinking about His holiness connects us with Him. Few of us would begin shouting to a friend whom we wish to visit while still six blocks down the street. Few of us would begin speaking to someone on the telephone before the connection is made. Yet many of us begin begging for all kinds of little human things before we have realized the one great divine thing which is His own holiness.

It cheers and cleanses our little souls to give thanks to Him for His own glory. It lifts us out of the sordidness of life to rejoice in the everlasting shining of His life of purity and power. It rests our striving spirits to dwell upon the resistless urge of the force that from everlasting to everlasting creates without motion and without sound.

But if we are very lonely it does not comfort our hearts. And so many of us are very lonely!

He has not left us comfortless. He has come to us, humbling Himself and making known His love to us through the love of man. Therefore the next step of our prayer, the step by which we translate the divine love into human terms, is for those of us who know Jesus to think of that most loving Son of Man, our friend. He stands before us when we think of Him, forever receiving the eternal life of God and forever transmitting that life to us through love. He has given us His name to use, as a human friend might give us his name to use when we approach a man greater than he. Let us then comfort our hearts by thinking of His human tenderness and love. Uniting our hearts with His heart (by loving Him), let us ask in His name that the life of God may be increased in us.

Finally, let us rejoice in the real and definite and perceptible increase of life within. For as we progress in spiritual power, we will probably perceive that life. We may be conscious of an inrushing current of energy, like electricity. We may feel this current of life renew our strength. We may feel pain or soreness disappear, consumed by the steady burning of God's light.

But before we have learned to perceive these physical sensations, we will be conscious of His entering into us upon the footsteps of peace. We will know by the stirrings of hope within our minds that He is there. And we will rejoice and give thanks for all those lovely gifts that it is both His will and His nature to give us—for He is love.

We give thanks for them because we believe that we are receiving them. Therefore we do receive them. For our joyful thanksgiving testifies to our faith, and through the doorway of our faith He enters in. How many Christians down through the ages have failed to receive the answers to their prayers by failing to take this last step—the step of giving thanks! God is standing before us with the answer in His hands. But unless we reach out our hands and take it by giving thanks for it, we are not apt to receive it. For while love is the wiring that connects our souls with His, faith is the switch that turns on the power. Our homes are full of things that run by electricity: lights, irons, sewing machines, toasters . . . Just believing that there is a power called electricity is not enough to make these things work for us. Every time that we want one of them to work, we must touch the button that releases the power in that one. Just believing a set of facts about God does not necessarily turn on the power in a single one of our prayer-objectives. In order to do that, we must believe that we are receiving the thing that we desire. If we really believe this, we will naturally rejoice and give thanks for it. And when our belief is weak, the act of rejoicing and giving thanks will awaken our faith.

Let us praise Him then, for His life in our spirits increasing in us the consciousness of being His children, light of His light, life of His life. And let us rejoice in His life in our minds, directing and arranging our thoughts, increasing our mental powers, giving us a better grasp of business and more wisdom in every line of work we undertake. Let us thank Him for His life in our hearts, ordering and controlling our emotions and filling us with His own love. And let us give thanks for His life in our bodies, recreating them after the image of His perfect health and strength. How easy this becomes when we know that our bodies are made of His own energy and full of His own light! How comforting to realize that when we expose our souls to Him in prayer, we absorb His life as simply and naturally as a leaf absorbs the sunlight! With infinite care He made the leaf so that every tiny cell therein can absorb the sun. With the same care He made us so that every cell within our frames can absorb Him. Therefore we need not hesitate to give thanks for each adjustment, however great or however small, that we would like His loving care to make in us.

"I give thanks that Thy life is now releasing tension in

my legs and taking away all stiffness," we can say. "And I give thanks that the shining of the Holy Spirit is restoring harmony and order to all the glands and organs of the pelvic region. I rejoice that at this moment Thy healing light is removing all pain from the spine and filling the back with new vigor and life. I rejoice that Thy perfect vision is restoring perfect vision to my eyes . . ." So one by one we can extend His blessing to everything within us that needs that blessing.

"Let everything within me praise the Lord."

How full of praise the Bible is! And how continually the apostles and teachers of Christianity urged us to rejoice always, in *everything* to give thanks!

They knew!

4

The Re-birth Of Faith: Re-educating The Subconscious

If the conscious mind were the only sentient force within us, the prayer outlined in the preceding chapter would probably be enough to make us well. But the part of us that reasons is only one-tenth of the consciousness. Psychologists tell us that nine-tenths of our thoughts lie below the level of consciousness. Moreover, it is this submerged part of the consciousness—this subconscious mind—that controls our bodies. A moment's thought shows us that this is true. In order to breathe, we do not have to think, "Now breathe in—now breathe out—now breathe in—now breath out." The breathing is regulated by an inner control center. This inner control center is part of the spiritual body, the eternal Being. It acts under orders from God Himself until man sends into it a contrary command and throws it into confusion.

If we desire to go here or there, we do not need to direct the nerves and muscles of the legs. The subconscious mind takes charge of them. It is like an engineer deep in the bowels of a ship. The ship goes forth to sea under the general order of the steamship company: to cross the ocean and land safely upon the other side. The engineer sets his engines to obey the general order. On his way across the sea he alters his course, increases or slackens the speed of his engines, according to orders sent him from the captain on the bridge. The engineer cannot read the captain's mind. He merely responds to the suggestions from the bridge.

So it is with the inner control centers of our being. Our little crafts go forth upon the sea of life under the general orders of our Head: to cross the deep waters of this life and land safely upon the other side. There is a hidden engineer within our bodies, placed there by God to see that we do this. The subconscious engineer acts under a blanket order from God, who is love and life and who gives us His love and bids us live. There is also a captain in our heads: the conscious mind, which enables us to cooperate with God in a reasonable way.

The engineer within the body cannot read the captain's mind. The subconscious mind does not respond to reason, but only to suggestion. Every time we think, "Oh dear, I'm afraid I'm catching cold," the subconscious mind picks up the suggestion, "Catch a cold." God has equipped the body with white corpuscles whose express purpose is to destroy enemy cold germs and so preserve the body in God's image and likeness of perfection. But the thought, "I'm afraid I'm catching a cold," sends a contrary order to the inner control center, which immediately telegraphs to the white corpuscles, "Slacken speed—slacken speed. The captain says, 'Catch a cold.' " Thus the natural resistive forces of the body are thrown into confusion, because they are acting under two conflicting orders. Their efficacy is weakened, and the body is much more likely to catch a cold. So by our own contrary thought-suggestions we constantly destroy the protective and life-building energies of the body.

Moreover the subconscious mind, psychologists tell us, keeps everything that we have ever stored within it. By the time we are middle-aged most of us have accumulated in the subconscious all manner of thought-suggestions of fear, illness, limitation and lack, every one of which is in direct contradiction to the voice of God. From their store-room of memories there floats into the conscious mind a continual stream of doubts, fears and negations. Hence arises the destructive inner voice that says, "Oh yeah? You think this will work, do you? You're trying to kid yourself, that's all. Now don't be a fool!" and such remarks. The Bible calls this inner tempter Satan, and states that powers of evil beyond the tangible forces of this world battle against us. The love-vibrations and the faith-vibrations of God enter through our thoughts of life and love. In the same way, the destructive thought-vibrations of Satan enter through our thoughts of illness, hate and death.

What are we to do about this?

Most of us will immediately think, "We must fight it! We must resist it!"

But this is precisely the wrong approach. If we respond to our doubts by thinking, "I just won't think that way! I won't, I won't," we increase the nervous tension and add to the thought-suggestion of fear. In other words, to fear of illness we will have added fear of our own thoughts.

Jesus did not contend with Satan. He merely turned His back on him. In doing so, He lived so far above evil that He was able to say, "The Prince of this world . . . hath nothing in me."

Indeed the power of evil has nothing on us if we turn our backs on it.

"Oh, *that!*" we can say to ourselves, when we notice our own negative thinking. "That's nothing. It's only the old thought-habit and hasn't quite faded out. I'm learning a new thought-habit and pretty soon I won't think that way anymore. But in the meantime it can't hurt me at all, because my real self is a child of God and so is full of thoughts of faith and power.'' And by an act of will we can continue to give thanks, quite unconcerned about the other voice that murmurs within us.

In so doing, we ignore the old thought-habit; we turn our backs on Satan.

But this is not all of the task. We must also gently and patiently teach ourselves a new thought-habit. We must re-educate the subconscious mind, replacing every thought of fear with a thought of faith, every thought of illness with a thought of health, every thought of death with a thought of life. In other words, we must learn faith.

How often we have heard a person say, ''I guess I just haven't the faith to get well.''

Of course we haven't! That's why we are learning it! One does not have mathematics at the age of six. But one can learn to add and subtract, divide and multiply. One is not born playing the piano. But one can practice five-finger exercises and drills and so learn it. We learn mathematics by studying its laws and then correcting every mistake that our pencils make. We learn music by mastering its fundamentals and then correcting every slip of our fingers as we practice. So we learn faith by trying to understand that we are children of light and then correcting every thought that denies our glorious heritage of life and love. This daily practice will gradually fill the subconsciousness with the new thought-habit of faith, so that one day it will overflow into our lives. When that day comes we will not need to correct our thoughts any more, for faith and peace and joy will be our instinctive and natural reaction to every situation. Surely this is worth a little mental training! If we desire to become musicians, we do not resent the daily drill. If we want to learn typewriting, we do not refuse to practice every day. Surely it is as important to learn to think with power as it is to learn to play the piano or type!

Therefore if we find ourselves thinking, "One of my headaches is coming on," we correct that thought.

"Whose headaches?" we say. "God's light shines within me and God doesn't have headaches!"

And we rejoice in the Lord and give thanks for His perfection that is being manifested within us. If our first attempt to do this does not succeed, what of that? The Wright brothers' first attempt at an airplane did not succeed. They tried again and again and again. Cannot we be as good Christians as they were scientists? Every time that we meditate upon God's life and light instead of meditating upon a headache, we are building into our inner consciousness a new thought-habit of health. Some day that new thought-habit will be stronger than the old one, and headaches will be no more.

If the thought, "Oh dear, I'm afraid I'm getting flu," crosses our minds, let us correct that idea right away.

"My nose and throat and chest are filling with God's light, and if there are any germs there, they are being destroyed immediately. I rejoice and give thanks, oh Lord, for thy life within me, recreating all my inner passages in perfect health."

If we find ourselves thinking, "Oh I can't possibly do that. I haven't the strength," we correct the thought.

"God's strength flows into me continually, and is sufficient for my every need. By faith I see my back and my limbs strong and tireless, and I give thanks, for so it will be."

Every prayer should end with this strong command: "So be it;" "Amen."

We should correct ourselves gently and patiently. We only lose time by becoming impatient with ourselves. For impatience or discouragement tightens the nerves and blunts the faculties, and we become more stupid than ever. We must be loving toward our own subconscious minds in order to control them. Indeed, we shall succeed much better by playing a little game with God, as Billy did, than by struggling with ourselves! Let us close our eyes and see ourselves holding the ball, running ahead of all the other guys, and then let us say, "Thank you, God, for that's the way it's going to be."

Or let us see ourselves walking down Main Street with our heads up and our shoulders back, with light in our eyes and a spring in our footsteps, and let us say, "Thank you, God, for that's the way it's going to be.

And gradually the voice of doubt will speak no more within us, and we will be remade in His image and likeness. This is the double method that Jesus Himself used to rout the power of Satan. He turned His back on him. And He was conscious always of the Father within, doing His own work.

This was not easy for the Master and it will not be easy for us. All sorts of questions will come to us. One of these questions is so common a weapon of Satan that it is worthwhile to mention it at this point. Here it is.

"What about St. Paul and his thorn in the flesh?"

St. Paul's thorn in the flesh has become a veritable thorn in the spirit to thousands of Christians, who take St. Paul as an example for cherishing illness. In this they are not consistent. If St. Paul were really their example, they could raise the dead. For in seeing him as an example of the invalid saint, they do the utmost violence to the Biblical picture of a man strong enough to endure shipwreck and exposure, stoning and imprisonment and still accomplish more than ten ordinary men could.

Behold the impressive roll-call of saints given in the eleventh chapter of Hebrews. Is there a weakling among them? Noah, who in his five hundredth year built an "ark" the size of a modern cargo ship; Moses, who at the age of one hundred and twenty stated that his eyes were not dim nor his natural strength abated; Elijah, who girded up his loins and outran the king's chariot horses; David, who slew a lion and a bear with his bare hands. There is no record in the whole Bible of a holy man who remained an invalid. Stories of illnesses we find, but these stories are almost funny in the portrayal of a tremendous urge toward health. The prostrated holy men were outraged at illness, regarding it as a sign of being cut off from God's love and cast out of His presence. From David (who made his couch to swim with his tears) to Job (who sat upon a dung-heap and cried unto the Lord till he recovered) we find no instance of an acceptance of illness as the will of God. Job is sometimes thought of as the type of a suffering holy man. Well he may be because he refused to submit to his boils and sought God day and night, in spite of the scolding of his wife who advised him to curse God and die, and the smug advice of his friends who suggested that he was not worthy of health. And he found God. He received an overwhelming vision of the holiness of God, a vision that transformed him from a comfortable righteous man to a seer and a prophet with health and prosperity.

Why should we ignore this glorious processional, led by the Son of Man, and accept a standard of imperfection? And why should we justify ourselves in this acceptance by the example of St. Paul, who overwhelmingly demonstrated the power of God?

What, then, of his thorn in the flesh?

Let us consider his thorn in the flesh with an open mind, and see if we can understand it. St. Paul had been miraculously healed more than once. He had shaken off a deadly serpent and felt no sting whatever from its bite. He had been stoned and left for dead, and had risen from under a pile of stones and walked into the city. He had accomplished the most amazing of miracles, even the raising of the dead. Yet toward the end of his ministry, he was troubled by a "thorn in the flesh." He prayed about this matter and God said to him, "My grace is sufficient for thee: for my strength is made perfect in weakness."

He did not receive an instantaneous healing. Instead of that, he received every day enough of the Grace of God for that day's needs. So do I. And if God's perfect strength accomplished through me as much as it did through St. Paul, I would be well content.

I was once called to a distant city to see a lady ill with a painful and "incurable" disease. She wrote me later that her pain was greater than ever, but that the inner voice of her Heavenly Father had directed her to rise from her bed and work. With unspeakable courage she did this. She went to her kitchen by resting upon each step until she had summoned the strength to go on. When she had reached the kitchen, after fifteen minutes of agonizing effort, she sat upon a stool before the sink and began to peel potatoes.

"I am peeling this potato in the strength of Almighty God," she would tell herself, while the sweat of desperate weakness dewed her face. "I can't exhaust His strength, because He is inexhaustible. So I will certainly and surely get this potato peeled, and for that, oh Lord, I do thank you."

When she had peeled one potato, she would drop into a chair and rest and then get up and peel another one. We had hoped that she would get well right away. But, like St. Paul, she did not. Instead she was told that His strength was made perfect in weakness, and by peeling one potato after another *in His strength*, she found out that His grace was sufficient for her. Today her thorn in the flesh troubles her no more. They say that her recovery is miraculous, for doctors had long ago given her up. Yet even today she would have little strength unless she fed continually on the ever-flowing strength of God.

If she had been as old as St. Paul, and if she had already overcome as much as he, her healing might have been completed in the next life and not in this. That would be a matter of comparative unimportance. The important thing is that by learning to feed upon the life of God continually for the renewal of her strength, she received, like Job, a new vision of His holiness and power. She peeled potatoes in His strength, she made beds by His power, she swept her house to His glory, and finally she ventured forth to help others by His love. In so doing, she came to know Him so well and love Him so sincerely that she gave thanks for everything. In weakness, she gave thanks for His strength overcoming the weakness. In pain, she gave thanks for His healing power working through the pain. At the gates of death, she gave thanks for His life in which she would forever live, both in this world and in the next.

If she had interpreted "My strength is made perfect in weakness" to mean that she should cherish the weakness, her lovely body would now be gone from this world, her children would be motherless, her husband sorrowing, and many sick or lonely ones she has healed or comforted would mourn for their lost friend. (And those well-meaning fatalists who call themselves "resigned" would sigh, "God's will be done.")

But she interpreted "My strength is made perfect in weakness" to mean that in her weakness His strength would be made perfect. She does her own work, teaches classes, starts prayer groups, attends conferences, prays for the sick and comforts the sorrowing by renewing her strength through His strength every day. And to many she has become "as an hiding place from the wind, and a covert from the tempest; as rivers of water in a dry place, as the shadow of a great rock in a weary land."

5

The Law Of Love

*The foregoing chapter suggests a two-way system of connect-*ing with the healing power of God. What if we practice this system and fail? Shall we doubt God? Edison did not doubt electricity when his experiments with the light bulb failed. Instead of that, he doubted the wires that he had used in making his light bulb. If we are sensible we will not doubt God, we will doubt our world and we will doubt ourselves. We will search our own souls to find the break in the pipeline of the water of life. And we will search our civilization to find the false standards that blind our eyes to God's light.

The children of a certain Bible school watched water flowing downhill through a trench into a hole.

"Is the water bound to flow downhill into this hole?" the teacher asked.

"Oh, sure!" the children cried.

"Why can't it change its mind and flow uphill?" the teacher persisted.

"Because of the law of gravity! You can't change the law of gravity!"

"Now let's find a lot of little stones and build a dam across this trench," the teacher suggested.

The dam was built, and the water was once more poured into the trench. It did not reach the hole.

"Now the water is not flowing into the hole," the teacher pointed out. "I guess the law of gravity can be broken, after all."

"Oh, no!" the children said, with complete faith in the law of gravity. "You can't break the law of gravity! We put something in the way of it, that's all."

"God sends you Himself—His own life—according to a law called love," and the teacher. "The Bible tells us that God does not change, and His law does not change. Then if you're sick and ask for His life, which is certainly able to make you well, and you don't get it, is it because the law of love has changed?"

"I guess not," puzzled the children. "I guess it's because we have put something in the way."

Sermons in stones, books in the running brooks! Every law that God made cries aloud of His unchangeableness, yet blind humanity insists upon doubting the pure current of His love instead of doubting the pureness of its own channels.

When the greatest Conductor of God's love appeared among men, He found these channels almost completely blocked by many things that were not love. The hate and fear and misery of man had built, as it were, a dam in the very air surrounding this globe, a thought-vibration of evil so powerful that the main current of God's love could not get through, as sunlight cannot get through a thundercloud. By His outpouring of love He broke that dam, and reconnected man with God, who is love. The men who were first reconnected with God and felt the inrushing of His power did the very works that Jesus did. They caused the lame to walk and the blind to see, the deaf to hear and even the dead to live. They were so radiantly and absurdly happy that men said, "What is the matter with these people? They can't be drunk! It's too early in the morning!"

They were so happy that they could not imagine ever giving in to old age or sickness or death. Jesus Christ had promised them that He would come back to them. It seemed to them that the only natural thing, the only right thing, the only possible thing would be for Him to return in time to save them from death. He had been, however, very vague about this return of His. He had seen clearly the final accomplishment of His purpose upon earth, and so He had stated from the shadow of the cross, "I have overcome the world."

What He knew, or what He felt it wise to tell them, He did tell them: that He would return to cooperate with them in His great redeeming project of sending forth love; and that finally this love-power would conquer the whole kingdom of Satan, and there would be no more death, neither sorrow nor crying, for all the former things would pass away.

He did return, in His Holy Spirit, at Pentecost, and so He returns to each of us today. But the completion of that returning, when His glory will shine from one end of the heavens to the other, the world has yet to see. He has accomplished His redemption. It is our turn next. We are His channels for the sending out of His redemptive love into the world.

We have not done this. Hence the break in the pipeline that carries His love to humanity.

Even the first Christians did not quite succeed in living up to His high standard of love, made perfect in His prayer, "Father, forgive them, for they know not what they do." He told them not to be angry at all, and upon the cross He showed that it was possible to live up to this. But even among the first apostles we find dissensions.

As the early Christians departed little by little from the high standard of Christ, the power of God faded away little by little from among them. Realizing this, they saw that the Kingdom would not come in their lifetime. Sadly they postponed their glorious vision of a new heaven and a new earth. Sadly they laid aside their hopes of being "clothed upon with immortality" and accepted death.

"Yet I am not ashamed," said St. Paul with unexampled courage, "for I *know* whom I have believed, and am persuaded that He is able to keep that which I have committed unto Him against that day."

As generation after generation passed, that day seemed farther and farther away. For still His people were waiting for Him, not realizing that He was waiting for them. Farther and farther away became the actual carrying out of His projects. For as century after century rolled by and the power of God dimmed out from among men more and more, they placed the responsibility for this dimming-out on Him and not on themselves. There came a time when the actual working of God's power was the exception rather than the rule, and man called it a "miracle." And after that, there came an age so dark that even the last resort of the sick, the sacrament of Holy Communion, was looked upon as the forerunner of death and men expected the Bread of Life to prepare them for death, never dreaming that it would restore them to life.

What a state the world would be in if we had adopted toward God's laws working in wood and water, stone and fire the attitude that we have taken toward God's laws working in air and spirit, flesh and blood! Can we imagine a caveman finding out that wood burns and then refusing to use wood as fuel and insisting that stone should burn instead?

Yet that is exactly what mankind has done regarding the fire of the spirit. Only love can generate a healing fire. The One who first generated it made this fact inescapably plain, both in His blunt and forthright teachings and in His tremendous demonstration of a love that held toward His tormentors even in the hours of death. Yet the Christian church abandoned love as its heavenly fuel, and began to insist that the stone of cruelty should burn instead. We do not like to think of the lengths to which they went in trying to make stone burn. They looked upon riches of the East and saw that they were great. Therefore they organized "Holy Wars" and got upon their horses and crusaded to Palestine.

Atrocities worse than the crusades were committed "for Christ's sweet sake": pogroms—inquisitions—witch burnings—and worst of all, the age-long persecution of His own brethren, the Jews.

And so the church, by doing in the name of Christ the very things that Christ told them not to do, lost the power to heal. Only the faithfulness of occasional holy men who appeared through all ages, and only the tremendous force of the love of God Himself, kept any power among men at all.

This want of conformity to the law of God, who is love, is our greatest sin. And if we wish to receive more of the inflow of God's love, we must learn to give more of the outflow of God's love.

A certain man had a faulty water system in his lakeside cottage. He knew that there was no lack of water in the hills. He knew, moreover, that it was in the nature of water to flow downhill into his kitchen sink. He did not stand before the faucet and cry, "Oh water, please flow into my sink." He looked for the break in his pipeline. He searched diligently and found it. Whereupon he uttered a whoop of joy. The source of the trouble having been found, it was then a simple matter to mend the pipeline so that the water could flow freely.

We have located a great break in the Christian pipeline of power—the forsaking, by the church at large, of the stern law of love. This should cause us joy rather than mourning, for having found the cause of the leakage, we have the remedy already at hand. We need only go back to the teachings of the Highest Authority on this subject, check them over carefully and adjust our lives to them, and we can once more open the valve to the water of life.

Jesus did not invent a straight and narrow way of life in order to make things difficult for us. He only made plain to us the original creative principles through which God works. These principles are built into our spirits, our minds and our bodies and neither Jesus nor anyone else can evade nor avoid them. They had been seen more or less dimly by religious thinkers of all ages. Jesus Christ restated them, however, with much greater force, outlining not only acts that we cannot do without danger to ourselves, but also thoughts that we cannot think without harm to ourselves.

"It was said by them of old time," declared this amazing carpenter, " 'Thou shalt not kill!' But I say that whosoever is angry with his brother is in danger . . ."

St. Matthew's account of this course of instruction reads, "Whosoever is angry with his brother without a cause." But Jesus could not have said "Without a cause" for in this very chapter He says again and again that one must forgive *no matter what the cause*. Was someone, copying the original manuscript, angry with his brother at the time?

Let us consider then, what the Highest Authority upon the subject of God actually taught about the law of love.

Jesus began with a warning concerning the danger inherent in this tremendous flow of energy. Danger lurks in every form of energy. The flow of energy that we call the law of love is the rhythm for which our beings were created, the thought-vibration in which we live and move and have our being. Every thought of anger, therefore, throws a contrary and destructive counter-vibration into the body, and places us in danger. "Whosoever is angry with his brother—shall be in danger of the judgment."

This judgment begins immediately. One of its first evidences is the failure of the prayer-power of the angry one. He will find that he cannot pray, no matter how hard he tries. He will also notice in his body the immediate results of anger. A fit of wrath destroys the appetite, upsets the digestion, weakens the muscles and confuses the mind. And the anger that solidifies into hate, resentment or hurt feelings deposits a continual sediment of poison in nerves, arteries, bones and mind, and prepares the body for death.

Doctors tell us that anger tends to destroy the body. Jesus said that it also tends to destroy the soul. "But whosoever shall say 'Thou fool,' shall be in danger of hell fire."

The words sound harsh, but they are true. For the forces of spirit, mind and body are synchronized and ordered by the same inner control center, and that which affects one affects the others. As long as the thinking of the conscious mind is in harmony with God, the subconscious mind directs the functioning of the body in a marvelous way. But as soon as we turn the dial of our thoughts to hate, bitterness, hurt feelings, resentment and irritations we send a contrary order down to the engine room of the subconscious which responds with the general order, "Hurt! Destroy!" The protective and life-giving forces of the body are weakened so that one falls prey to germs and infections, to pain and weakness, to nervousness and ill temper, and to the spiritual dullness that results from the dimming of the life force. If one looks with an open mind upon the history of war and epidemics he will perceive this fact.

The One who knew, therefore, was not harsh nor was He dealing in fantasy. He was only realistic as He stated, in His own blunt, straight-from-the-shoulder way, a fact that cannot be evaded; the one who is angry with his brother is in danger.

Christians have tried so hard to avoid this unavoidable law! Their excuses for anger range from the "righteous indignation" that slew the unbeliever to the "righteous indignation" that thunders against modernist or fundamentalist or Catholic or Jew. But there is no way of side-stepping the law of God, because it is written in our own subconscious minds. And the subconscious mind cannot figure out the difference between "righteous" and "unrighteous" indignation. Its working is inexorable and absolute, founded on laws set in motion before the foundation of the world, and no puny excuse of man-made mind can change it from its course. A man might drink poison in ignorance, mistaking it for water. In so doing, he would be acting righteously. No blame could possibly be attached to him. But that would not prevent the poison from destroying him. Therefore the Teacher, who was a most profound psychologist, told us that the poison of hate is dangerous, no matter what the cause of the hate may be.

Jesus suggested a very sensible method for avoiding the danger. "Agree with thine adversary quickly," He said, "whilst thou art in the way with him; lest at any time the adversary deliver thee to the judge, and the judge deliver thee to the officer, and thou be cast into prison. Verily I say unto thee, thou shalt by no means come out thence until thou hast paid the uttermost farthing."

Just so. Lest one thing lead to another—lest a sense of superiority lead to hurt feelings and hurt feelings lead to insult and insult lead to war; lest anger lead to stomach ulcers and stomach ulcers lead to cancer and cancer lead to death; let us agree with our adversary quickly, upon our first encounter with him. Let us avoid every possible cause of anger. We would be wise to direct our lives as much as possible toward paths of peace. We would be wise to plan our food, rest, work and recreation in as healthful a way as possible in order to soothe and harmonize our beings. For much of our bad temper springs from no other cause than weariness and over-strain. We would also be wise to take the wrath-provoking words and acts of other people as assignments from God, as spiritual exercises, or as helpful hints along the way of life rather than as excuses for anger.

I recall visiting a very dear elderly lady who needed prayers for healing. A young lady, equally admirable and fine, happened to arrive while I was there. The conversation had been steered toward healing and in course of time the invalid asked the young lady whether she attended my lectures on this subject.

"No, I don't," responded the younger woman with all candor. "I tried it, but the dogmatic, opinionated way she talks annoys me."

"I can see there's truth in that," I said. "I'm so anxious to get across my point that I guess I do come down on it in a pretty flat-footed way. I'll try to improve along that line."

It is such fun to learn and to improve, to correct and to heal! And it is no fun at all just to be angry! For eventually one is delivered to the judge of one's own body and one must pay to the uttermost farthing.

Not all spiritual adventures, however, are without pain. There are those who would strike one upon the cheek or steal his coat or compel him to go a mile with him as a burden-bearer, as the Romans did to the Jews. There are those, in other words, who would insult, defraud or bully one. The human answer to this problem is self-defense. What did Jesus have to say of that?

Alas! He showed a way that very few have learned. He instructed those who would follow Him into that happy and powerful life, the kingdom of Heaven, to practice forgiveness rather than revenge. They were not only to love those who deserved to be loved—their friends. That was easy. Even the heathen did that. They were also to practice love toward their enemies. He suggested that when struck upon one cheek, they turn the other cheek toward the angry one; that when defrauded, they give to the defrauder; that when bullied, they perform an extra service for the bully. Those who have taken these suggestions

literally and tried them out have found them to be the most
perfect methods of self-defense.

And we become perfected in love by trying to do it. The
method is so simple that any child can learn it. It is merely
to connect in spirit with the love of God, send that love to
the other person, and see him re-created in goodness and
joy and peace.

"Wow! I never saw anything work like that in my life!"
cried a little girl, to whom I taught this method. "Before I
got up this morning, I lay there and thought of my Mom
like she is when she's all happy, and I said "Thank you,
God, because you love her and you're making her like
that now.' And then I thought that way about my Dad,
too. And my Mom, she came up and kissed me and she
smiled so nice I just stood there and looked at her! And my
Dad, he pulled out a quarter and said, 'Here, go and have
a good time, Kid.' Wow! I never saw anything like that in
my life!"

A certain engineer was once surveying in a field when a
bull charged his party with lowered head and thundering
hoofs. There was no tree to climb. There was no fence to
jump. So the engineer stood his ground, filled his mind
with the love of God and projected it to the bull.

"I am God's man and you are God's bull," he thought in
silence. "God made both of us, and in the name of Jesus
Christ I say that there is nothing but loving-kindness between us."

The bull stopped abruptly. For a moment he looked
about uncertainly, as if confused. Then he wandered off
and lay down peacefully under a bush. And all that day as
the men prospected in the field he grazed quietly behind
them, as if he enjoyed their presence.

"Will you tell me what you did to that bull!" asked a
farm boy who was holding the rod for the surveyor. "That
was a mad bull if I ever saw one. *Will you tell me what
you did to him?*" ("I can believe every story in that book

except the one about the bull," a lady once said to me. But the engineer was my brother, and the story is true.)

The farm boy had seen, for the first time, the working of that force that will eventually take the place of bombs and shells upon this earth. For as soon as enough people are able to use the power of love in such a way as to create thereby a perfect self-defense, wars will be outmoded. When one can obtain justice and right and friendly cooperation without money and without price, without bloodshed and without pain, it will no longer be sensible to fight for them.

"If an armed burglar broke into your house with intent to kill," the old question goes, "what would you do? Fight him, or lie still and let him kill your wife or child?"

Silly old question. One would do neither. One would project into the burglar's mind the love of God, by seeing him as a child of God and asking God to bless him. And if one were strong enough in faith and love, the burglar's mind would change. He would leave the family unharmed and go away.

"But hardly anyone can do that!" the answer comes.

Obviously. For if we could, we would not need to resort to war in order to defend ourselves. And we had best learn to do it, for until we do, we must suffer. Until we know the method of love and brotherhood, our choice of weak non-resistance or self-defense is only a choice of evils.

A new age is being born. The day has come when love-power, at the command of ministers and surveyors and children and everyone, is sufficient to change hearts here and there in the world about them.

This is the beginning of a new order. It is the dawning of a new day!

6

Re-education In Love

There are those who will not believe the story of the
surveyor and the bull, just as there are those who do not
believe the old story of a prophet in the lion's den. But if
the reader really wants to find out whether love has such
power, he can do so by the simple process of learning love
and trying it for himself. In order to do this, he must
re-educate his subconsciousness. He must form new thought
habits of love and compassion and friendliness and joy, so
that his instinctive and natural reaction to every situation,
every person and every animal may be one of love.

This is not difficult. It is easy, because it is working in
harmony with the laws of nature. It seems difficult to us at
first. But this is because we have not taken it as a serious
assignment from God. We have dismissed it as unnecessary,
coolly setting aside what Jesus came to tell us about it. In
fact, we have formed habits of dislike toward certain
people or races or rulers or sects which we have no
intention of giving up. We are almost as absurd as the lady
who remarked that she didn't like spinach and she was
glad she didn't like spinach because if she liked it she
would eat it and she didn't want to eat it because she
didn't like it. We are apt to feel that we do not want to like

certain people because if we liked them we would be friendly to them and we don't want to be friendly to them because we don't like them. In other words, the real reason why most people do not learn Christian love is quite simply that they do not want to do so. They deny this, of course, saying, "Oh, but I really have nothing against anybody," or as one minister naively remarked of another, "Oh, I love him with Christian love, but I don't *like* him."

Christian love is the love of Christ, an energy so overwhelming that it led our Lord to give His life for His friends, and to give it with a joy that carried Him through untold anguish. The debasing of this real human-divine tenderness, its demotion to a third-rate state of feeling of mild affection, its reduction to a vague goodwill is not the victorious love that we have been seeking!

What, then, is Christian love? It is a powerful, radiant and life-giving emotion, charged with healing power both to the one who learns to love and the one who is loved.

To some people, this great love comes as a free gift from God, but most of us need to learn it. And how can one learn it? By practice. If we think that a daily drill in forgiveness is worthwhile, let us select a time and place for this exercise and hold to it. Our Lord suggested that we retire into a "closet," or private room for prayer, and close the door to all outside distractions. This simple act demands untold courage! When first we undertake a program of prayer, the adversary seems to cause every possible interruption to come at that very moment. The postman arrives at the front door and the laundryman at the back door, the telephone has delirium tremens and the coffee pot boils over.

Upon such little things do the great matters of life depend!

For our success or failure, our health or illness, our triumph in love or our defeat by hate will depend upon that tiny effort of attention by which we think clearly concerning our choice; shall we keep the appointment with God, or shall we set it aside in favor of the laundryman? True, the laundryman makes more noise than God does, but if we are to put God first we must plan accordingly. If the laundry is outside the back door, the laundryman will collect it and go in peace. If it is not, he will quite justifiably raise a horrid din until we come to the door.

Life is so ordered that we cannot pray successfully without the harnessing of our intelligence and our will power, so let us first deal intelligently with the laundry so that we will be able to deal intelligently with God.

Then let us follow the four steps of prayer suggested in chapter three: (1) *relaxation,* (2) *meditation upon the reality of God,* (3) *asking for the indwelling of God's life,* and (4) *giving thanks for the increase of power within.*

Let us think of the person whom we have selected for the day's assignment and hold up this person before the mind, surrounding him with the light of God's love. Some of us see in our minds the picture of Jesus Christ and then see the other person, placing the picture of the one we would forgive upon the picture of Christ. Having done this, we say to the one whom we would learn to like, "I forgive you in the name of Jesus Christ, and I give thanks to God because you are now forgiven. Amen." And we rememeber that "Amen" means "So be it," and is therefore a command sent forth in the name of Christ.

The name of Jesus Christ adds power to all prayer, but most particularly to the prayer of forgiveness. For all forgiveness is of Him, and as we forgive we merely permit Him to carry on through us that great work of setting men free by love for which He came upon this earth.

Having once accomplished a forgiveness in His name, we must never question it, lest we stop the work that He is doing through us. Having said, "I give thanks that so-and-so is forgiven," we must keep on giving thanks that this is so. We must trust the actual working of God through us, and must not be misled by our own unruly feelings. The feeling toward the forgiven one may not immediately change. Indeed, that sense of revulsion and coldness that is the forerunner of death may be even more noticeable for a day or so. This is because we have dragged the half-forgotten dislike out over the threshold of consciousness, and like pulling up a tree by the roots, it throws up a lot of dirt. Therefore we need pay no attention to our feelings, knowing that they are only the result of an old thought-habit of irritation and that they will soon pass away.

If a doctor removes a cinder from the eye, the discomfort may not go immediately. Indeed, the eye may feel worse for a few minutes. "That's all right," the doctor may say, "your eye is still sore because it has been irritated for so long. Forget it." So when the name or face of the person whom we have forgiven comes into mind again, perhaps with the usual irritation, we ought to think, "That's nothing. Jesus Christ has forgiven so-and-so through me, and therefore she *is* forgiven, no matter how I feel. That feeling is only the old thought-habit, and it will soon go away."

We then proceed to the second step of forgiveness, which is to say, "I bless so-and-so in the name of the Lord," and to look with expectancy for the changes that the Lord's blessing will accomplish in her.

This will require practice. Until the new thought-habit of love becomes stronger than the old thought-habit of dislike, we must patiently correct each uncharitable thought that passes through the mind and replace it with a thought of love.

One of my friends once rushed up to me with a beaming face and announced, "I can say the Lord's Prayer at last!"

"What do you mean?" I inquired.

"All this time I haven't been able to say any further

than 'Forgive us our trespasses,' because I still didn't like Jane Harmon. But I've learned to like her! Honest! It took me a whole month to do it, but I have! It used to be that I wouldn't go over there when school was out for fear I'd see her. But this month I've purposely gone over there when I knew she'd be home, and tried being nice to her and seeing her sweet and friendly and good. It used to be that I'd duck into a store when I saw her coming down the street. But here lately I march right on. The first time I did this, I had to make myself smile. 'Smile, woman,' I said to myself. 'After all, you're supposed to have the adult mind around here. Now you smile if it kills you!' But now I don't have to do that, because I just naturally smile. And you know, come to find out, she's really a good kid. Honest she is!''

What tremendous power would be poured out upon the earth if every Christian would so learn to earn the right to say the Lord's Prayer!

When we have triumphed in prayer as this woman did, we will be apt to see the goodness in the other person, for his hidden goodness probably will be brought out and strengthened by our prayers. Jane Harmon actually did become more friendly and more sweet, and how much of that was due to the prayers of her friend, only the Lord knows.

I learned this method by experimenting with my own children. When one of them came in cross and unhappy, instead of flying into a temper, I would quiet myself and by faith make in my mind the picture of the child as he was at his best. "Heavenly Father, that's your little child as you want him to be," I would say. "Please send your Holy Spirit through me now and make him be that way, happy and peaceful and kind. Thank you, because I believe you are doing so. Amen." I would then hold firmly to the picture of the bright-faced, happy child whom I wanted to see. And in less than a minute, the child would change and the thing that I had seen in my mind would be brought forth.

We are indeed made in His image and likeness. He is first of all a Creator—and so are we. The more we practice the work of creation the more easily and naturally His power works through us. After a few months of practice, I found that my prayers could influence my children by "remote control," as my daughter expressed it. If I heard angry voices anywhere in the house, I had only to make in my mind the image of a child at peace and project it into reality by the word of faith. And after a time, this work was accomplished and there was no more need to think about it, for my children lived in peace together from day's end to day's end.

"Blessed are the peacemakers," said the Teacher.

The creation of peace in someone else, by projecting into that one the love of God, is true forgiveness, the remission of sins, the changing of the other person, so that the quality in him that has annoyed us will not be there any more. If we really try forgiveness we find out for ourselves that this is so, for people sometimes change before us in a most amazing way.

I once outlined to an intelligent and open-minded mother this method of changing someone through God's love.

"What can I do about my little girl?" the mother asked. "She is the strangest child—she never smiles! She worries and worries because she thinks she isn't pretty and people don't like her. She isn't very pretty, really; she's so scrawny and thin. But she'd look prettier if she smiled . . . And the worst thing is, she doesn't seem to have any affection for me or anyone else. She thinks I don't love her. Of course I do, but she *does* make me cross! What can I do?"

"Stand beside her when she's asleep and lay your hands on her," I suggested. "This gives you the closest possible connection with her, as you no doubt found out when she was a tiny baby, and you could soothe her with your hands. Then say to yourself, 'By faith I see my child loving and happy and open-hearted and well, as God made her and wants her to be. And in the name of Jesus Christ, I say that this shall be.' ''

"Amen" would have been another way of saying "This shall be," but I put the affirmation in the modern words, knowing that the mother would not have understood the meaning of "Amen."

"But I am not a Christian," the mother stated with admirable frankness.

"Then try it anyway," I said, hoping that as she worked in harmony with God, who is love, God would help her whether she knew Him or not. "Make the picture of the child as you want her to be, and say, 'My love brought this child into the world, and through my own mother-love I re-create her after this image!' '' And I left in some trepidation.

A month later I saw this lady at a meeting of the PTA.

"It worked," she beamed. "I never saw anything like it in my life! The next morning Susie came to my bedside and smiled, and said, 'Good morning, Mother,' and kissed me! And she's been like a different child ever since! She's happy, and she's gained weight and she's much prettier!"

I need not have wondered whether it would work. God is always much more broad-minded than I am. Two years have passed. The results of this prayer-experiment have continued to grow, and both mother and daughter are now Christians.

There is no more joyful thing in all the world than an act of love that sets free the forgiveness of Christ in another. The first step in forgiveness is the overcoming of resentment, that is, learning to like someone whom one has not liked before. The second step, which should follow spontaneously and naturally upon the first, is the re-creation of the forgiven one by love. Having forgiven someone, we do not see his faults any more. Instead of that, we see his virtues, creating in our minds by faith the exact opposite of the traits that has annoyed us in this person, and projecting them by faith into reality. These good and happy traits will often rise to the surface and be manifest, as if they had been there all the time only awaiting the touch of love to bring them forth. This does not always happen, of course. Some people's minds are closed so tight that love seems to beat against them in vain. But even in cases like this, love may plant a seed in the mind of the forgiven one and that seed may bring forth fruit sometime, somewhere.

The one who prays thus is like a gardener. When he pours out upon his fellowman the forgiveness of God he often sees that man come to life as a parched plant comes to life when water is poured upon it. And seeing this, his faith is increased. For the sake of our own joy and faith, then, let us practice sending forth the forgiving love of God not only toward those whom we have learned to like, not only toward our irritating children and the problem people around us, but also toward any person whom we see in need. If we try this as a solemn duty, it may not work. Prayer needs wings of joy to fly upon. But if we do it happily and spontaneously, as a sort of game, we will often see it work right before our eyes.

On one of my most joyful and therefore one of my most powerful days, I entered the elevator of a tall city building and an employee entered after me. She stood with her back to me, but I knew by every sagging line in her body that she was depressed.

"How you doing, sister?" asked the elevator boy.

"Oh-h-h—tired before I begin!"

"I bless you in the name of the Lord," I thought. "I see you as a child of God, strong and refreshed and joyful, for through my prayers His strength is entering into you."

The girl's bent shoulders lifted immediately. "I dunno!" she cried to the elevator boy in quite a different voice.

"Maybe life's not so bad, after all. I got a hunch today's going to be a good day."

The elevator door opened and she tripped down the corridor lightly, head held high. She had come to life more rapidly than any plant can come to life when water is poured upon it! The living water had entered into her and through the sending forth of human compassion, projected by faith, had forgiven her sins; that is, had set her free from the result of her own un-godlike thinking. For God is life and love and joy, and she had been thinking lifeless, unhappy and loveless thoughts. How long it was before the force of the old thought-habit brought back her weariness I do not know. But my thinking had released her, at least for the moment. And how much better to ease our fellow-beings as we walk among them by our own joy and light than to burden them with the extra weight of our crossness and depression.

"Ye are the light of the world."

There was a strong church-woman whose life was ruined by resentment toward a son-in-law.

"I don't want to dislike him!" she lamented. "I spend all day trying to forgive him. But he has turned Mary entirely against me, and I just can't stand it. I'm not really angry with him, but I'm so *hurt*—and I just can't go on this way! I can't eat and I can't sleep and I'm a wreck!"

She learned the way of forgiveness outlined above and we practiced it together. The first result of this forgiveness was to ease her own heart and so restore her own health. A second result was to change the heart of the son-in-law. His home was thousands of miles away. The mother made no move at all except the move of forgiveness. But since the kingdom of Heaven knows no limitations of time and space, the force of her forgiveness, projected across a continent, touched secret springs within the hearts of both daughter and son-in-law. They re-opened a correspondence that had been dead for many months. In the course of time they moved east. The sympathy and understanding between the two families grew continually stronger. So the mother was restored to her daughter and was increased in love toward all people and in power to help the sorrowful. And the son-in-law developed into a more warm-hearted and unselfish person.

Perhaps this is what the Teacher meant when He told us, in His simple, homely way, that we should be like salt. Salt does not insist upon its own flavor, but brings out the natural goodness in everything with which it comes in contact. And we, by sending forth the forgiving love of Christ, can bring out the natural goodness in those we meet. For every living creature tends to return love for love.

A snake once crawled near me as I lay on a mossy bank in the woods seeking to know the reality of God's life through the sunlight. It did not occur to me to scream or to run, for I was conscious of oneness with God and therefore with the snake which God had made. A bee once tumbled against my face, touching me again and again as I weeded in the garden.

"Listen, you," I said aloud, "I love you, but I'm busy. Now go climb into a hollyhock." And so he did.

"With what measure you mete, it shall be measured to you again," said the Teacher.

It is even so. We learn to give forth love in learning to forgive our enemies. Then we learn to give a forgiving and healing love to all who cross our paths and need our love. Finally love flows through us spontaneously and naturally to both man and beast—and completing the circuit, flows back to us again from God.

7

In The Shadow Of His Wings

As we practice the work of forgiveness we discover more and more that forgiveness and healing are one. We find indeed that all forms of prayer fuse into a high consciousness of God. Thus the break in the pipeline that connects us with God who is love is mended, and the water of life fills us to the brim and overflows into our homes and workshops and churches.

This inrush of God's Holy Spirit heals us—naturally. But it does far more than that. Indeed, as we pursue the spiritual life we lose sight of physical benefits in our increasing vision of God Himself. We find after a while that we desire God more for His own sake than for ours. And as this comes to us we begin to understand a little bit of that process by which the world will be filled with the glory of God as the waters cover the sea. More and more we seek the beginning within us of the manifestation of the sons of God who will walk the earth with power, accomplishing the works of Him who sent them. More and more surely we know that the day of the Lord, when nation shall not rise up against nation neither shall they learn war any more, can only be brought about by us, the children of light.

So we learn to cure our diseased bodies by seeing, in our own flesh, God. And in the end we offer up ourselves, both flesh and spirit, to God for His purpose: the bringing in of the kingdom of God on earth.

"In my flesh shall I see God," remarked a very wise man of ancient days.

Could he have meant the literal perception of the light of God within the framework of flesh?

Anyone who has seen an X-ray of his foot has seen his foot in a different light. It is seen not as a solid and impenetrable thing covered with skin but as a shape made up of light, the bones being merely a shadow in that light.

"But that is not the reality," we may say.

Why not? We are seeing the foot illuminated by a greater light. Why may not that more intense light-vibration show as true a reality as the naked eye can see? Science tells us that it does, for the body is mainly made not of matter but of energy, open and penetrable to the various forces of the air. Sunlight penetrates the open spaces of the body. The vibrations of electric treatments can be sent through apparently solid flesh. The light of X-ray and radium shines through the body as easily as if it were made of light itself, as indeed it is.

And above and beyond all these, a spiritual light-vibration penetrates and fills every cell of the body. In other words, we are porous like a sponge and filled with God.

"As a sponge is in the ocean and the ocean is in a sponge," Rufus Moseley once said, "so we are in God and He is in us." Or as another wise man expressed it, "In Him we live and move and have our being."

There is a parable concerning two little fishes who met a frog beneath a rock.

"Don't you know you're in great danger, little fishes?" croaked the frog.

"No!" cried the fishes, much frightened.

"Don't you know fishes can't live without water?"

teased the cruel frog. "You'd better find some water quickly or you'll die."

The little fishes swam to their mother in great distress.

"Oh Mother, Mother! The frog says if we don't find some water quicly we'll die! Mother, what's water?"

"I don't know," confessed the mother fish, who was an agnostic. "I never heard anything about water. Let's go and ask the otter."

"Water, my dears?" laughed the otter. "Why, you live in water! That's what you breathe!"

We live in God. That's what we breathe. And this is so whether we know it or not. But we can absorb either more or less of His life-force according to the receptivity of our spirits. Most of us have so closed down our spiritual gills that very little of it flows through us and our flesh stagnates and hardens for lack of life. We call this process of stagnation and hardening "old age." Sometimes this stagnating flesh decays more rapidly in one spot than in another or is attacked by parasitic growths, as all stagnant matter is apt to be attacked. We call this sudden and rapid deterioration of life "illness."

The remedy for all of this is more of life and light. And it is precisely the inflowing of more light and life that we receive through our health-prayers and our acts of forgiveness. This spiritual life stimulates the circulation, relaxes the nerves and releases the natural bodily energies. It also strengthens and invigorates the mind and causes the thinking to flow more quietly, strong in the peace which is the result, not of lessened activity, but of heightened activity. Moreover, it increases the spiritual perception, so that we are aware of the workings of God not only in our bodies but in the world around us.

All of these results take place gradually, in the normal manner of growth. The inflow of life should be so free and powerful that a minor disorder such as a cold very quickly disappears. But the rebuilding of the body following a chronic disorder nearly always takes time, and requires that combination of open-minded patience and unfaltering courage that the Bible calls "meekness." I found this out by experimenting with a condition of my own that required corrective surgery. The "operation" has been performed gradually and imperceptibly by the re-directing of the creative forces of the body. My daily prayers for healing removed temporarily the aching and weariness due to this condition. But I found upon examination that it had not corrected the collapsed organ nor removed cysts. At this point I toyed with the idea of an operation, but decided that as the condition was not dangerous to life, I would first try every other resource. My own prayers having been insufficient, I requested help from a distant prayer group and from my friends at home. With this additional help, I began to perceive as I prayed for healing a drawing-up sensation and a distinct vibration and warmth in the lower abdomen. Moreover my increased vigor and relief from pain indicated that a process of rebuilding was taking place. After some time I went back to my doctor for an examination, in order to find out what had taken place. He was rather cross.

"I told you to come here twice a week for treatments," he scolded. "And I haven't seen you for a year."

"Well—I've been busy."

"You look good," he admitted in a cold, suspicious voice. "What have you been doing?"

"I haven't seen any other doctor," I evaded.

"You've certainly been doing something," he insisted when he made his examination. "You're a hundred per cent better. *What have you been doing?*"

I tried to tell him, but was obliged to desist when he began to exhibit symptoms of apoplexy. He had seen the results of a daily prayer for health assisted by the prayers of others. But he could not understand. He was so accustomed to dealing with the envelope of flesh that he could not see the body through the X-ray machine of the spiritual eye.

If I had given up on finding that my own prayers were not enough, this gentle and gradual healing would not have been finished. Many a healing is not finished simply because the one who prays does not hold his faith long enough, and in most cases I find that it is necessary to maintain faith, because the healing takes place gradually. However, in the follow-up prayers one may pray with thanksgiving rather than with pleading. "Thank you, Lord," we may say, "your power is working in this person toward a perfect healing. Continue therefore to use my faith as a channel of power until the healing is completely accomplished." One may then renew in his mind the picture of the person completely well, and try to keep that picture bright and clear until it has become reality.

However, in the case of accidents to myself, I remind myself of my real being as a child of God, and His light that shines in me continually.

As we do this something shifts within us almost as rapidly as a car shifts into high gear. We leap immediately to a spiritual platform of peace and safety. For instance, I once slammed a very heavy door upon my finger, turning it black. If I had said "damn" and had fought the sickening pain, the finger would have continued to hurt. But being very conscious at the time of my own power and authority as a child of God, I held my finger up before Him and blessed the pain therein, congratulating it as one of His healing agencies.

The pain ceased instantly, as if I had somehow shifted my sensations over into the spiritual kingdom where there is no pain. How it came to pass I do not know, but a tiny hole appeared at the base of the mashed nail and all the black blood seeped out of it. The nail resumed its normal color and kept it, suffering no ill effects whatsoever.

Being a speedy and casual cook, I have many a time

spilled boiling fat on my hands while officiating over the stove. If I do not lose my temper, the hand is not burned. One's reaction to boiling oil is exceedingly speedy. And if one gives way to temper first and allows it to burn, it is too late then to remove the burn by prayer, for by that time we are delivered to the judge of our own inner consciousness, which in faithful obedience to the thought-suggestion of fear and wrath has directed the hand to burn. "Agree with thine adversary *quickly*," said that most profound of psychiatrists, knowing the tremendous power of the first thought-suggestion sent down into the body. It is unnecessary to stop frying potatoes and pray. We have already prayed for the indwelling of God's Holy Spirit. Let us then act upon it, assuming the dominion that is ours as children of light and assuming it in any simple words that come to mind. My own thoughts at such times would be quite unacceptable in any book of prayers, for I am apt to meditate in kitchen language. "I'm boss inside of me," I'm apt to think. "And what I say goes. I say that my skin shall not be affected by that boiling fat, and that's all there is to it. I see my skin well, perfect and whole, and I say it's to be so."

"But that's not a prayer at all!" one may object.

No. I have already been charged that day with the power of God's indwelling life, so it is not necessary to ask for it again. I am assuming it and acting upon it, and my remarks are the following-up of prayer, inadequately expressed by a busy woman who must cook, clean, wash, iron, raise children and befriend a parish, and cannot be on her knees all day. All thoughts of power, conscious or unconscious, are the follow-up of prayer—the rounding out of our prayer-work in our lives. The woman who thus controls a finger that has encountered boiling oil does so in the sure knowledge and feeling of God's power within.

My son, in the Navy's officer training program at the

time, once expressed his method in an even less churchly manner.

"I had a terrible sore throat and chills and fever," he said. "But I wasn't going to go to sick bay and take castor oil like the rest of the guys, and that's all there was to it. So I remembered the way you do things, Mom, and I didn't do it exactly that way, but I just made up my mind, *'To hell with this!'* And I went on to classes and drill and football practice, and it got all right."

This form of meditation is not recommended. But the Holy Spirit, who as a very holy man once said, has "a sacred and subtle sense of humor," could not have been displeased at the young man's remarks, for the cold disappeared. Perhaps He who knoweth our frame remembered that the boy was in the Navy. . . .

As our prayers, our mental training and our acts of forgiveness fuse into a high consciousness of God's indwelling, we become more and more aware of an inner source of power that can be tapped at will. We also become more and more aware of an outer source of power: a protecting and guiding influence that surrounds our day's work with blessings and guides us into paths of peace.

As Gerald Heard says, "God is both transcendent and immanent. And His immanence is the key to His transcendence."

In other words, God's light shines both within us and without us, and by learning to receive Him within we begin to perceive Him without.

This being so, let us gladly seek Him without as well as within. As we fill our beings morning after morning with His light, let us also fill our days with His over-ruling guidance and help and protection. Let us give thanks that His power is working not only in us but also in the world outside of us. Let us bless the day through which we are about to walk and lift it up into the light of His love. Let us invoke His blessing on everything that we intend to do during the coming day, as many Jews bless each step in the baking of their bread. And if we do not know what we should do that day let us offer it to Him, asking Him to use it according to His will. Sometimes He has His own plan for the day, and for that reason we have been unable to make one.

On days that we have given Him we must be particularly quick to hear and heed His voice, lest we miss the very opportunities that He is sending us. For the Holy Spirit that spake through the prophets speaks both through us and to us today, in the kindliest possible manner, and we need only still ourselves to feel His presence.

I once made the above statement to the children of a daily vacation Bible school. A small friend of mine, being very wise, rushed home and tried it immediately in order to find out whether or not it was true.

"Don't bother me, Mother," said he. "I'm going up in the attic and try one of Mrs. Sanford's experiments."

The mother, knowing her offspring, awaited his return in some trepidation.

"Well, it worked," he announced cheerfully, bounding down the stairs. "Mrs. Sanford said if you thought about God a while and then made sure you weren't mad with anybody and then asked God to tell you something, He would. Sometimes you'd hear it like a little voice, and sometimes you'd just feel it."

"What did you ask Him, Buddy?"

"Well, you know, Mom, I *did* want to go swimming today—"

"Oh-oh!" thought the mother, who had just nursed Buddy through measles. "He's going to tell me God says he can go swimming. *Now* what am I supposed to do?"

"So I asked Him," continued Buddy serenely. "And I heard Him just as plain! He said, 'No, Buddy, not today.' "

"To think I'd doubt Him after all He's done for me!" said Buddy's mother, on telling me the story of his conversation with God. "But Buddy's such a tough young one, I never thought God would talk to him."

We are continually amazed and delighted that God will talk to us, that He loves us, that the guiding Intelligence of the universe really cares for our small concerns. His lavishness overwhelms us and His humility humbles us. For as nothing is too great for Him, so nothing is too small.

Every day of my life proves this to be an actual fact. For on the days when I am in harmony with God, who is love, all things both great and small seem to work together for my good. My work is done easily and with power and my decisions are quick and unerring. Everything "clicks," in other words. But when I fall into annoyance and irritation, nothing "clicks." I work slowly, make careless decisions and waste time generally.

In all these tiny ways I find that a meditation which began for the purpose of healing had become really a prayer for at-one-ment with God, or harmony. By daring to try God and see whether His promises are true, I have regained a measure of that instinctive faith of the very young or the very simple.

There is a story, told to me as truth, that so beautifully illustrates God's encircling protection that I shall relate it, although I cannot prove its verity as I can prove the verity of the other stories in this book.*

In the First World War there was an English woman whose son was a pilot in the RAF. This mother became greatly afflicted by a recurrent nightmare. She dreamed that she was walking in a meadow bordered by poplar trees and sloping toward a little stream. It was a lush green meadow, dotted with daffodils. As she walked among them, she heard the sound of planes. She looked up and

---

*After this book was published, a letter from England definitely confirmed this story.

saw them, an English plane and a German plane. She watched a battle between them. The English plane crashed to the earth, and burst into flames. She ran up to it and dragged out the charred body of her son.

Such was the nightmare, from which she would awaken drenched with sweat and in an agony of fear. Again and again she was tormented with this dreadful dream, till all her waking thoughts were heavy with the fear of it. At last, fearing that she would lose her mind, she sought help from a psychiatrist.

"I will tell you what to do," he said. "Think about the highest thing you know. If you are a Christian, think about God."

"I think I'm a Christian," answered the woman.

"Then think about God. Think of Him as light and love and protection. Then think of your son, and see him at his very happiest and healthiest and best."

The woman trained her thoughts moment by moment to follow this pattern of thinking. So the light and the love of God became real to her, and in that light and love she placed her son. As she so reordered her thinking, the nightmare came to her less frequently and with less horror. Gradually her daytime fears decreased. She noticed, moreover, a changed feeling toward her son. She had always loved him, but now she loved him more than ever. She forgot the little things in him that had worried her, and dwelt joyfully upon his best and happiest characteristics. Finally she ceased entirely to dream about the lush green meadow and the airplanes, and put the whole matter behind her.

Some months later she was at a houseparty in the south of England, and went for a walk in a meadow. Suddenly she looked about her with a start of amazement. For it was the meadow of her dream! There were the poplar trees and the little stream—and there were daffodils in the grass, for it was spring. Almost immediately, she heard the sound of planes. She looked up and saw them—an English plane and a German plane! She watched a dog-fight. One of the planes fell and crashed into the meadow. But it did not burst into flames. Out of it stepped a young man, perfectly unharmed. He ran up to her, his face radiant.

"Mother!" he cried. "The most wonderful thing has happened! I knew I was falling, and I wasn't a bit afraid, and on the way down—something in me seemed to wake up—I just felt different!"

The reader may reject this story if he likes. I cannot prove it, any more than I can prove the chariots of fire about Elisha, the pillars of cloud that led the Israelites across the wilderness, the vision of Joseph that bade him take the young child and his mother and flee into the land of Egypt. But I thank God that I am able to believe all these beautiful and thrilling stories of a God who gives His angels charge over us, to keep us in all our ways.

But one thing in this story is plain and clear to me: the mother lifted herself out of her fear by surrounding the one she loved with God's light and life. In so doing, she not only overcame her fear. She also made it possible for a guiding Providence to protect her son from a death that would otherwise have been inevitable. This, thank God, I can believe, for I have helped to do the same thing for many a boy in danger.

"But isn't it selfish to pray for the protection of your own?" some people ask. "Some boys have to be killed!"

This is a foolish question. It is as if a mother said, "Isn't it selfish for me to feed my baby because some babies have to starve?"

But where are we to begin if we don't begin with those that God has especially given us to protect and pray for?

Let us then begin where we are, praying for the protection of our own and trusting the transcendent God to weave these prayers together in His own time and His own way toward the protection of us all.

"But if everybody prayed like that, how could we ever have a war?" some people ask.

The answer to that is simple; we couldn't.

Those who seek God for the protection of their own are not working selfishly. They are among the makers of the coming peace. They are beating a path through the wilderness of life toward the kingdom of Heaven. And this straight and narrow path shall one day be the broad highway of all humanity.

8

Doctors, Ministers And God

If every one of God's little family upon this earth lived constantly in harmony with Him, there would be no more pain, neither sorrow nor crying, for all the former things would pass away. The Old Testament story of creation holds out to us this unbelievable possibility. If all men could only live securely in the light of God and never absorb into their beings the results of knowing both good and evil, men could live above death and above the illness and pain that lead to death.

One plain fact I dare to state: as more and more of us see God, live in harmony with Him and show forth His perfection in our bodies, minds and spirits, the "normal" processes of growth, maturity, old age and death will be altered. It will be possible for one who daily receives from God his spiritual sustenance to live without illness or decay for a longer and longer period of time. The Bible from first to last is full of these promises, which we have for the most part disregarded. "They that wait upon the Lord shall renew their strength; they shall mount up with wings as eagles"; or as St. Paul more boldly states, "For this corruptible must put on incorruption, and this mortal must put on immortality."

My own experience and observation demonstrates the fact that these promises are true. Those who learn by daily meditation and practice to become "new creatures in Christ Jesus" are actually renewed in strength and youth.

At present, however, this *final* victory has not come to pass. Though we are one body in Christ (many members in one body, all partaking of the common humanity in which the love of God is pleased to dwell), we still share the weaknesses of humanity. If we keep our hands ever so clean, they may still be affected by some poison from without, entering the body through another member, the mouth or a scratched leg or an infected sinus. So even while we are trying our best to live as children of light, we may still pass under the shadow of the world's sorrow and reflect it as illness. The receiving apparatus of our subconscious mind picks up such a high voltage of pain-suggestions from the outside world that at times it weakens the bodily defenses and we fall prey to disease. True, the more foot-sure we become along the path to Heaven, the less this is likely to occur. But when it does happen, we only waste time in reproaching ourselves. It is more sensible to use the illness instead as a means of learning more about God. When the disciples asked Jesus whose fault it was, this man's or his parents', that he was born blind, Jesus refused to consider the question.

"Neither," He said, ". . . but that the glory of God should be made manifest in him." And He proceeded to manifest the glory of God in the man's condition by restoring his sight.

So when in spite of all our efforts toward life and health we become sick, let us take it as an opportunity of manifesting the glory of God by getting well, as Jesus did. He showed forth the glory of God always, in every single instance, by healing the sickness; never by allowing it to continue.

We are almost sure to find that the very first step of

prayer, the realization of God, is impossible when our minds are clouded by illness. God is light and joy and peace, and we are at the time in darkness and sorrow and discomfort. So it is very hard for us to create within us the glow of knowing that we are part of His eternal life. And as for giving thanks that we are showing forth His life and perfection, how can we when we aren't?

He knows that we cannot. He knoweth our frame, He remembereth that we are dust. And so He has most kindly provided a number of ways of helping us when we cannot adequately help ourselves.

Let us not be ashamed to accept healing from another when we cannot find it by our own efforts. We are not too proud to go to God's servants, the clergy, for our spiritual help. Why should we be too proud to go to God's servants, the doctors, for our physical help? There are those who in their enthusiasm for spiritual healing put it in place of both church and the medical profession.

Surely they lose by so doing! My own adventures in prayer for healing have brought new life and spiritual power into my church and have made me a better Episcopalian. But I would never think of putting meditation and mental training in place of the services of the church. Religion is far richer and deeper and broader than one's daily prayer for the indwelling of God's life, important as that prayer may be.

Nor do I see any need for refusing to cooperate with God by availing myself of any physical aids toward health that I know: rest, exercise, proper diet, and if necessary, medicine. Medicine stimulates the bodily forces, inspiring them to do the work that God made them to do. If I were sufficiently full of the life of God, I would not need this stimulation, true. But if I were, I would not be sick.

Being sick, therefore, I gladly call for my best friend and adviser, the doctor. He not only helps my body, he also helps my mind. His cheerful assurance strengthens my faith, and his diagnosis calms my fears. I should not have fears, true. But I do have, and there is no fear so destructive as a fear of the unknown. No one can pray with power while thinking, "Oh dear, I do feel awfully queer. I wonder if something terrible is the matter with me?" The time will come, of course, when we do not think that way. But let us not despair of ourselves if at the beginning our faith bends beneath the harsh winds of pain.

All things are of God. The antibiotics, for instance, are a source of power implanted in nature for man's use, just as electricity is a source of power implanted in nature for man's use. An occasional ecstatic prophet tells us that in the course of time the glory of God will so fill the earth that there will be no need for other forms of illumination. Maybe so. But in the meantime, we are grateful for electricity. We hope that in the final working out of God's will, the kingdom of Heaven on earth, the light of God will shine so radiantly through all mankind that there will be no need of other forms of healing. But if we contract appendicitis or typhoid in the meantime, we had best be grateful for the physician. To insist upon getting well by our own efforts in such a case might be a gesture of faith, but it is equally likely to be a gesture of spiritual pride. Moreover, it is hardly kind to the family who must look after us nor to the doctor who must pick up the pieces if we fail.

If the voice of the Spirit within tells us insistently that we need no help but prayer, then we must heed that voice. But unless our guidance is *overwhelmingly sure,* we had best call the doctor and cooperate with him in humility and trust, knowing that God will bless our work with him. Perhaps God knows, not only that the faithful mind needs help from a doctor, but also that the doctor needs the strengthening example of a faithful mind.

There is a lady of a very loving heart who through faith brought Christ into a hospital.

She once told me that her abdomen was getting larger and tighter all the time, although she tried her best to "work on it" by prayer.

"There must be something wrong with my faith," she said. "Because that swelling hasn't gone down a bit."

"There's nothing wrong with my peach tree," I told her. "It's not bringing forth fruit yet, but it's growing. Your faith is younger than my peach tree, and it's growing too. But maybe the thing you want it to bring forth is too big for it. If I wait two or three years, my tree will bear peaches. But in the meantime, if I want peaches I'll buy them at the market. If you wait two or three years, maybe your faith will be big enough to heal a growth like this. But in the meantime, if you want healing, you'd better get the doctors to help you."

"Maybe I had," confessed the lady with a giggle. "I've kidded around about this as long as I can. Mamma said, 'What's the matter with you Nan? You're getting awfully fat around the middle!' And I said 'Oh, don't you know? I'm going to have a little baby.' Of course Mamma, she didn't believe that at my time of life. But I just sort of put her off . . . But now I don't feel good, and she sees it. So I thought if you'd put your hands on my stomach and say a prayer for me it might get well."

"I will, if you're willing to pray for guidance and to do anything that God wants you to do to help Him make you well."

We prayed together, and she waited for guidance. As the days passed, her peace of mind and her general strength increased. But "Ella May," as she named her growth, also grew in size.

"That's your guidance," I told her. "It's just as if God said, 'All right, Nan, I'll make you well. But I want you to let my friends the doctors help you.' "

"Why?" she demanded. "Lot's of people get well by faith alone, even if they've got something as bad as this."

"I don't know why," I confessed. "But I'm sure God wants you to go to the hospital."

She went to the hospital and stayed three days. At the end of that time, a solemn group of doctors surrounded her bed and pronounced their verdict.

"We cannot operate," they said. "Your growth is far too advanced. Moreover, your heart is weak, your blood count is very bad and there is sugar in the blood stream. There is not a chance that you would live through the operation, and we cannot take the responsibility of performing it."

"Praise the Lord," beamed their patient, "because I didn't want an operation anyway."

"Now you just put your hands on 'Ella May' and pray," she told me, "because God will have to get me well without an operation."

"I'll pray, and I believe you will get well, and we will leave the method up to God," I replied.

In three months her heart and circulation were perfect, but her growth was larger than ever. Her perplexed doctor once more made arrangements to send her to the hospital.

"This is beyond me," he fumed when he finally located her on the day before her hospital appointment. "Where have you been all day?"

"In Philadelphia buying a gas stove," said the patient cheerfully.

"I thought I told you to rest!"

"Oh, but I was resting," she beamed. "I was having me a good time. And I really do need a gas stove."

The doctor threw up his hands in despair. "I just don't get it," he said. "You've no right to be on your feet at all in your condition. Yet you go to town and shop all day, and your heart and pulse are perfect."

"The Lord's done it," said the patient simply. "But He hasn't done a thing about the growth, so I guess He's waiting for you to help Him."

Her doctor went with her into the operating room. When the surgeon made the incision, under a spinal anaesthetic, her doctor "turned green in the face," as she expressed it.

"Now you stop worrying and sit down in that chair," the patient directed him. "God and these hospital doctors are going to fix me up fine."

And while the "hospital doctors" toiled for three hours over a tangled mass of gangrenous growth, the patient encouraged and reassured them. "You just do the best you can and God will do the rest," she told them. "So now, see, you don't have a thing to worry about."

The next day I found her smiling and cheerful, though her face felt very hot.

"I'm all right," she said. "God and the doctors done fine. You don't need to pray for me. But let's you and me pray for a poor young thing down the hall there. Yesterday she went on something terrible. I heard her hollering and hollering and I asked the nurse about her. 'She won't bother you long,' said the nurse. 'She's pretty near gone. In fact, they've got the stretcher by the door now, waiting to take her out.' Can you imagine, dearie? Why, she's just a young thing, with three little children! 'God don't want that little thing to die,' I told the nurse. 'She'll soon be better. You'll see.' So I laid here and prayed for her, and dearie, she is better. She's stopped hollering, and they've taken the stretcher away from the door. So you help me pray for her now."

Together we held her up in the light of God's love and asked our friend Jesus Christ to stand beside her bed and lay His healing hands upon her.

Two days later she was well.

"She's sitting up in bed putting red polish on her fingernails!" cried Nan.

"And how are you?"

"Oh, I'm fine. The doctors said I had peritonitis that next day, dearie. But it's all well now."

"I thought you felt hot! Why didn't you tell me?"

"Oh well, I knew it would go away. And I wanted you to put your mind on that poor young thing down the hall. Dearie, the doctors don't know what's struck this hospital!"

No one knew what had struck that hospital. The poor young thing, whom neither of us ever saw, was discharged within a week. She did not know that the Friend of all men, sent through the love of an unseen woman, had stood beside her bed. Or perhaps she did know. Who can tell? And on all that hospital floor there was such light and joy that fears were calmed and broken hearts were healed.

"Maybe that's why God wanted me to go to the hospital," said Nan. "He needed one of His friends there."

"I'm sure of it," I replied. "You've helped the doctors as much as they have helped you."

So, if while we are striving to learn to live in God's perfection we fall prey to illness, let us not waste time in vain self-reproach or weak spiritual pride. Let us take the illness as a further opportunity of showing forth the glory of God. And if we need the doctor's help in overcoming the illness, let us rejoice in the opportunity of helping him by courage and faith. A large part of any doctor's work is the arousing in his patient of the will to live. Anything that the doctor can learn from the example of a healing speeded by courage and by faith will be a help to many another patient. Even if the doctor merely says, "Look at Mrs. Smith. She had something ever so much worse than yours, but she never gave up for a moment. And now she's well!" the patient has given the doctor a life-preserver to throw to other drowning folks.

So if God makes plain to us that we need a doctor, let us rejoice in the opportunity of cooperating with him. Let us bless his medicine and take it in the name of the Lord. Let us bless the doctor himself, so that he may be guided in helping us and we may be guided in helping him. For of all men on earth, the doctor will be most benefited when he comes to understand in full the marvelous power to heal that God has given him.

Having placed ourselves in the doctor's hands, however, let us not cease to work with him and with God by faith. Let us give thanks continually that God's life is within us, restoring us to health. Let us make a picture in our minds of that perfect health that we expect, and receive it in advance by faith. If our minds are too confused by illness to follow our usual four steps of prayer, let us compose one sentence of thanksgiving and repeat it over and over until the subconscious mind is full of it. This chosen affirmation should radiate the thought of health in a positive a statement as our questioning minds will accept.

I once caught a heavy bronchial cold which did not stop immediately upon the prayer of faith, probably because of some forgotten disharmony in my life. I therefore fell back upon the method of affirmation. It would have been impossible for me to say, "There is no such thing as a cold and therefore I am well." My mind would not accept any such statement. However, I knew that the very air I breathed was full of the radiation of God's power and that therefore I was breathing in life continually. I also realized that as I kept my mind open to this inflowing perfection of God, my breathing was bound to fall into the rhythm of His perfect health. So I was able to say, believing, "I am breathing in the life of God with every breath, and therefore I give thanks for perfect breathing."

For about an hour I repeated the phrase over and over, calling my mind gently back to it whenever the thinking strayed to other things. At the end of that time the breathing was so much better that I rose and went about my business, forgetting it. By nightfall it was well.

In ninety-nine times out of a hundred, the wise care of the doctor and our own perseverance in faith will raise us to life again. There is, however, the hundredth time—the sudden and deadly infection that is beyond the doctor's power of healing, or the slow and hidden deterioration that has exhausted the recreating power of the body.

Is there anything more that we can do?

There is. The most powerful healing method of all, we have not yet tried: the method of healing by the faith of someone else who acts as a receiving and transmitting center for the life of God. This is the oldest of all methods of healing, and it is the simplest. It is the method that Jesus used, and that He taught His disciples to use. He interposed His whole being between God and the patient, so that He might be used as a channel for the life of the Father, who alone, He said, accomplished the works. Many fervent seekers after prayer-power give God only their spirits, feeling that their bodies are unworthy of His use. They try by thought alone to arouse the spiritual understanding of their patients. This is beautiful. It may be, as they say, the "highest" way. But so many poor little people are unable to grasp through their pain the idea of perfection! Jesus in His loving kindness lent God not only His spirit and His mind but also His body. He felt "virtue" go out of His body when a woman touched His robe in faith. Those of us who follow humbly in His footsteps know precisely what He felt, for we have felt it too.

He was not content to mention someone's name before the altar or to send them "absent treatment." He nearly always went to see them. He gave them not only His spiritual understanding but also His tender human love and His warm and lifegiving bodily presence. He laid His hands upon blind eyes and deaf ears, that the currents of His own life-vibration might flow through His spirit and mind and the nerves of His body into the bodies of the sick. Thus He was able to heal not only those who grasped the idea of perfection but all of the little helpless ones who came to Him for healing, whether they understood what it was all about or whether they did not. Many of those were so spiritually awakened by the inflowing of God's life that they became new creatures in understanding. But some did not. In fact, some of them thought so little of it that they did not even return to thank Him. Nevertheless, He healed them because He loved them. And He gave His followers a training course in this type of healing and sent them out on missions to preach and to teach and to lay their hands upon the sick and heal them.

Most people of today are ashamed to offer themselves to God, both soul and body. They feel that He has no use for their bodies, forgetting the infinite pains that He took to incarnate Himself within the veil of flesh so that He might from that time forth enter into all humanity.

Many people of today are unwilling to recognize the operation of a spiritual power through the being (body) of man because they feel that it is unscientific. No one would have believed a few years ago that an orchestra playing in Boston could be heard and seen in Florida. They would have said that such a thing was unscientific. Yet it was not contrary to the laws of nature. It was only a bit in advance of man's understanding of the laws of nature. So it is with that power of God that works through the being of one person for the healing of another. It is not really "unscientific," at all. It is only the channeling of a flow of energy from God's being through man's being. It is the entering in of the Holy Spirit of God through the spirit of a man, via the conscious and subconscious mind of that man, via the nerves of his body, via the center and thence to his mind and his spirit. This message is sent, not from the level of the healer's mind nor even from the level of his spirit, but from the Spirit of God Himself who moves in a mysterious way through the spirit, the mind and the body of the one who prays into the body, the mind and the spirit of the patient. Thus he makes of his whole being, spirit, mind and body, a receiving and transmitting center for the power of God. He offers and presents to

God Himself, his soul and body, as a holy and living sacrifice, which is his reasonable service.

Although people do not understand this method of healing and profess to disbelieve it, they nevertheless use it continually because it is the instinctive method of love. Almost everyone who calls on a sick friend lays his hands on him in love—pats him or strokes his head or holds his hand with a vague feeling of imparting comfort, friendliness or peace! We need only to combine this homely human touch with the prayer of faith in order to work what the world calls a miracle. Time and again, even without understanding, this combination has been made by sheer blind faith and a miracle has resulted.

There was a minister whose child was born dead. The minister held up the tiny, lifeless form on his two hands and prayed. Whereupon, his two hands providing a perfect channel for the inflowing of a strong current of life, the child breathed and lived.

Had he merely knelt beside the baby and not laid his two hands beneath the tiny lifeless form, I venture to guess that the child would not have lived. In which case the minister would have concluded that it was not God's will for him to live.

God works immutably and inexorably by law. Until mankind learns and keeps the laws of life, God's will cannot be made fully manifest. He has never from the beginning until now healed anyone by the interposition of an arbitrary or capricious force. But He heals continually *by the addition of a higher spiritual energy to a lower physical energy*. Doctors call this "nature" and confess that they cannot always predict what nature will do.

There was another minister who was once called upon to baptise a dying baby, six months old. By the time he had reached the house in his buggy over the winding mountain roads, the child had been dead for half an hour. He was laid out upon the parlor table and surrounded by weeping

women. When the young minister looked upon the child
and its weeping mother, he had compassion on them. And
the love of Christ speaking through his mind bade him
baptise the child, living or dead.

As he began the baptismal service the feeling came to
him that the child would live again. Therefore he placed
the women upon the far side of the room and stood between them and the baby. Shielded thus from observation,
he laid his hands upon the child, dropped a little water into
its mouth and stroked its tiny throat. The child's flesh began
to grow warm. Toward the end of the baptismal service,
the child opened its eyes.

So he restored the child to its mother, even as Elisha
restored to the Shunammite woman her only son. And not
knowing why he did so, he used not only the sacrament of
baptism but also his own body for the conducting of God's
life into the child.

Seventeen years later, this minister visited the town
again and inquired after the child.

"Why, there he is!" said his host, pointing to a sturdy
lad of seventeen teaching a Sunday school class.

It had been God's will from the first that this child
should live. But had the minister not trusted the guidance
of the Spirit and sensed the healing power latent in the
baptismal service and in the touch of his own hands, the
child would nevertheless have remained lifeless.

It is natural that both of these stories should concern
ministers. Every minister is consecrated for God's service,
and only ignorance, fear of prejudice can prevent his being
used for healing. Even that cannot always prevent it. Mr.
Richard Spread, in *Stretching Forth the Hand to Heal,*
tells of his own awakening to the power of God. One of
his parishioners came to him in an advanced condition of
tuberculosis and insisted that he pray for health. Mr. Spread
was loath to do so, being unaware at the time of the power
of prayer to heal. Being unable to refuse, however, he laid

his hands upon the patient and prayed for his healing. To his complete amazement the patient was healed in a way that he could only call "miraculous." Many an open-minded minister has been brought to believe in healing through the faith of a parishioner. My own husband has often been called to baptise a "dying" baby. Not one of them has ever died. So he is now sure that the interposition of the sacrament of baptism together with his own person between God and the baby is sufficient to recharge any child with life.

The most simple, the most direct and the most powerful method of healing given to man is this method, used by Jesus Himself; the method of praying one for another, the healthy for the sick, the loving for those who need love, the strong for the weak. The logical person to minister this healing love of God is the minister, whose name itself indicates the nature of his calling. So if we encounter illness upon the road to health, let us call, not only for the doctor, but *also* for the minister. And let us pray that God may use the combination of our faith and of his consecration to set free power in both of us. Let us pray that our healing may be furthered through the act of humility which we offer in calling him and through the interposition of his office as priest. And let us also pray that our recovery may increase his faith, and that some word that we may be guided to say may encourage him in ministering to God's little ones upon this earth.

9

Being The Lord's Instrument For The Healing Of The Sick

Before the discovery of the vaccine for smallpox many a person died of this disease who might otherwise have lived. Before the perfecting of the sulfa drugs many a person died of pneumonia who might otherwise have lived. One cannot say that such deaths were God's will. If they were His final and ultimate will, He would not have provided for mankind the potentialities of vaccine and drugs, only awaiting the intelligence of man to harness and use them.

In the same way, many a person dies today, in spite of medicines and the ministrations of the church, for lack of a believer in healing sufficiently powerful in faith and love to charge the body with the healing spirit of God and project that power into the body of the patient. My own work has proved this again and again.

"Mamma, Fred's father's dying!" my little boy once said in frightened tones. *"He's dying right now!"*

And I knew that my child expected me to rush to the rescue of his playmate's parent. I was not keen on doing this. Though I had never met Mr. Williams, the children's chatter had acquainted me with his condition. He had had a rheumatic heart for many years, and would often come home at night so weak from exhaustion that the children would have to drag him from his milk truck and help him into the house. And he had just been seized with a second attack of rheumatic fever and had persisted in his milk route fearing that if he once gave up he would never work again. His wife, moreover, with whom I exchanged flowers and gossip over the back fence, had told me that he was a good man but he didn't hold much with this healing business. . . .

However, I could not bear the distress in my child's eyes. So I heaved a sigh, marched through the hole in the back fence and tapped upon my neighbor's door.

There was no answer, so I opened the door and went in.

I found Mr. Williams on a chair in the living room, slumped over a table, unconscious and breathing in a very strange way. I could not see his face, as it was buried in his arms. I sat down on the arm of his chair, slid one hand underneath him and placed my hands above and below the heart. It was beating precisely as the kettle drum beats in Strauss' "Death and Transfiguration"—insistently, irregularly, terrifyingly. (I found out later that the heart had swollen until it filled almost the whole chest and that every valve had burst and was leaking like a sieve.) However, at the time I needed no doctor to tell me that his condition was serious, for my own fingers reported it to me.

As soon as my hands were firmly upon his heart, I felt quiet, serene, in control. Forgetting the heart, I fixed my mind upon the presence of our Lord and invited Him to enter and use me. Then, Mr. Williams being quite unconscious, I talked informally to the heart, assuring it quietly that the power of God was at this moment re-creating it and that it need labor no longer. Finally, I pictured the heart perfect, blessing it continually in the name of the Lord and giving thanks that it was being re-created in perfection. Soon I could feel the heart beats becoming more quiet and regular. I could even feel the strange inner shifting that reports the rebuilding of flesh and tissues. The heart would become for a moment almost normal in its beating. Then again it would shake the unconscious form in agitated pounding. Whereupon I would quiet it again as one would quiet a frightened animal, feeling it almost as a living thing with a certain intelligence capable of responding to suggestion—as indeed it is. "All right, now," I would think. "Just take it easy. Easy now—easy does it. Just beat quietly and slowly. You don't need to labor. You're going to be all right. Easy now—easy."

Any doctor could learn to do this. He could on occasion control the heart of a patient by prayer without even explaining his method. "Be quiet," he could say if the patient were conscious. "I want to listen to the heart." And he could place his two hands upon the heart, bend his ear over it, and ask God to use him as well as his medicines for the healing of the patient.

I was not in the least afraid of Mr. Williams' heart, which I felt quiet and obedient between my two hands. But I was somewhat afraid of Mr. Williams himself and of his reaction when he should awake and find himself in the embrace of a strange woman. However, I need not have been. He awakened as quietly and simply as a child, and when I said, "I've been saying a prayer for your heart," he merely replied, "Thank you. It's much better."

Mrs. Williams, true, looked a bit startled when she rushed back from her neighbor's telephone to find her husband holding quite serenely to this healing business when she had said that he wouldn't.

By the time the doctor came, the patient had walked upstairs and gone comfortably to bed.

"Why, *Williams!*" cried the doctor two days later. "Why, Williams! What has happened? Your heart has gone back to its normal size!"

In this case, prayer with the laying-on of hands was the

specific remedy for a wrecked heart. If there had been no one to administer that remedy, Mr. Williams would undoubtedly have died.

"But if God had wanted him to live, why didn't He just heal him?" some people ask. God wants us to have electric lights. But He will not put them into a house without the help of an electrician. God has graciously endowed us with the dignity of free will. He has not chosen to make us automatons, whom he can jerk about with strings. He has given us minds, presumably that we may use them.

There must have been many a lovely child, dead of diphtheria, whom God longed to heal. One can imagine Him saying to a beseeching mother, "Yes, I want to heal your child. And I have provided in this world two means of healing her. One of them is anti-toxin and one of them is the even more powerful remedy of My healing vibration set free through the being of man. Let man find one of them or both of them, and your child will be healed."

God has made ample provision for our every need. He has supplied for almost every disease two specific remedies: one inherent in the properties of nature and discoverable by science, and one hidden in the being of man and discoverable by faith. But man must make the effort to find them, harness them, and use them. God will not feed us forever with the food of life. We must learn how to feed ourselves. It may seem cruel to a howling infant when a mother refuses to shove its food into its mouth, in order to teach it to use a spoon. But the infant is not the best judge of the mother's methods. Nor we of God's. "Shall the clay say unto the potter, 'Why dost Thou make me thus?' "

Surely, we have a responsibility beyond that of merely receiving the life of God. Surely we owe it to God and to mankind to go one step further and learn how to pass on this life to others. We owe it not only to God and to mankind, but also to ourselves. For unless we become transmitters as well as receivers of the divine current, it will cease to enter into us.

Those who understand the laws of electricity know that in order to keep a continual flow there must be a completed circuit. The energy that flows into a light bulb must be able to flow out and return whence it came. If the wire within the bulb is broken, the current can no longer enter the bulb. Those who observe the flow of water see that in order to keep clean and fresh the water must have a continuing channel. A lake has not only a source but also an outlet. Without an outlet it tends to become stagnant and unhealthy. So it is with the living water of the Spirit of God, the everlasting light of the heavenly electricity. We have learned how to receive life from Him. In order to keep that life flowing in us, we must now learn how to give that life to others. This is not a matter concerning which we have any choice. A light bulb cannot choose whether its wire shall terminate at a certain point or whether it shall not. If the wire terminates within the bulb itself, the current ceases to flow.

This working of the law of love perplexed me greatly for a while.

I found that those who came to me for help received at first a tremendous inflowing of power. This power should, I felt, increase as their understanding increased. In some cases it did so, but in other cases it tended to run thin as time passed. Searching for the reason for this, I perceived that those who continued to receive were those who felt gratitude and who expressed that gratitude. The ones in whom the life-force dwindled were those who merely asked and accepted with no thought of return. Some of these were very dear to me, being the spiritual children to whom I had given birth. But I found no way of circumventing the law that Jesus stated in so many different ways—the law that as we give, so we receive. This law is not arbitrary nor willful. It is written into the very nature of things, and we can no more alter it than we can alter the law of gravity. God's life is a flow—it is a living water—it is active electricity—it is love vibrating at a definite wave length and intensity. In order to keep this current flowing through us, we must give it an outlet so that it can complete its circuit. If we do not do so, the channel of its flow becomes clogged and it runs more and more thinly and finally ceases altogether.

Many people make a little spiritual progress and then cease to benefit from the very power that had been their joy and strength. They have received as much as they can receive until they learn to give—and they do not want to give.

The manner of giving is less important than the feeling of gratitude that makes one long to give. Those who from a spontaneous feeling of gratitude give of their money to further the ministry of the church keep their channels free for God's life. Those who give in loving service to others also keep their channels clear.

"I'm so grateful for what God has done for me!" one woman cried. "And do you know what I've decided? I have decided that in return, I'm going to try to make my husband the happiest man in the world!"

That was *perfect*. And as long as she consciously offered in loving service to her husband a thank-offering for God's loving service to her, she continued to receive from God the gifts of health and peace. She also received, over and above, an abounding love and gratitude from her husband.

"It's so hard to give anything to God!" she complained. "He gets ahead of you every time! Do you know that? My husband just follows me around and thinks I'm the most wonderful thing in the world! It's no longer any effort to make him happy—so now I'll have to think of another way of showing God how grateful I am."

So it is. The love of God rushes into us so eagerly that

one channel is filled and in order to keep His life flowing through us we must open another channel. Jesus knew that it would be so. It was for our own sakes as well as for the sakes of those who need us that He commanded every one of us, His followers, to go into all the world to tell people about Him—to heal the sick, to cleanse the lepers, to raise the dead. "Freely ye have received, freely give." And even that one who gives a cup of cold water in His name will not fail to receive His reward.

The parable of the talents teaches us that we are to give according to our ability. As we grow in understanding and in faith our ability should increase continually. Therefore the measure and quality of our self-giving should increase. God is pleased, at first, with the simple gifts of our humanity, the sharing of our time and money and of our human love. But when He feels that we are able to receive it, He will probably give us such an abundant flow of the water of life that we long to share with others the very faith that we have received. He will so fill us with His love that our hearts are touched by the sufferings of humanity and we cannot rest unless we share the healing love of God.

If we have no desire to share this love, we are in danger of losing all that we have gained. For the very essence of the Christian life is the giving of self to God. And we give ourselves to Him by giving ourselves to His children here on earth. "If ye love not your brother whom ye have seen, how shall ye love God whom ye have not seen?"

"He that loveth his life shall lose it. He that hateth his life for my sake and the gospel's shall keep it." Strange paradox! We come to God that His love may recharge us with life. And He recharges us so abundantly that our own lives are nothing to us compared to the joy of giving Him to others.

Yet it is not really a strange paradox at all. It is only the law of growth—of maturity—of bringing forth fruit. Nothing in creation is allowed to remain static. Why should we alone be permitted to continue to receive life without bringing forth fruit? An acorn planted in the ground does nothing but receive life at first, life from the earth, from the rain, from the sunshine. But very soon it begins to produce life, and this life changes as it grows. First it brings forth roots, then shoots, then leaves and finally more acorns. Moreover, it is not allowed to keep its leaves nor its acorns. It gives its leaves to the ground when autumn comes, in order to enrich the ground. As long as it continues in this cycle of receiving and of giving, it grows. If at any time it ceases to bring forth leaves and acorns, the lifeforce within it dwindles. And unless something is done to revive it, the tree will die.

So it is with us. He who created our lives fills us with the desire to re-create the little broken ones upon this earth. And if we do not feel that desire, then something within us has been blocking God. We have lived for ourselves so long that we have formed a thought-habit of selfishness, which is a sure forerunner of death. In order to set ourselves free from this inhibition, let us re-educate ourselves in giving. If the desire to give has not come to us naturally, let us produce it by an act of will. Let us discipline ourselves in the giving of our money and of our time, so that the greater desire, the desire to give of our very selves, of that life-flow that has meant life to us, shall come to us in due season.

"But I don't want to be a healer!" we may think.

It is not necessary to "be a healer." It is only necessary to learn to pray for others as effectively as we do for ourselves. Every Christian prays for others. It is not possible to worship in any church without taking part in prayers for others. We must learn to do so in a way that brings results, that is all. For there are ways of praying for others that are merely empty words, and there are ways of praying for others that set free power to heal, to redeem and to protect.

The easiest way of praying for others is the way that most of us profess to disbelieve and that most of us instinctively use—the personal-contact method. Through learning how to help people directly, face to face and often with my hands upon them, I learned how to help them by the more conventional method of intercession. Through understanding the few simple suggestions made in this chapter, the reader will more readily understand the method of intercession outlined in the next chapter.

Therefore, I present first a simple human way of becoming a receiving and transmitting center for love-healing by the laying-on of hands. It is a natural impulse to hold the fevered hand—to soothe the aching brow—to pat the fretful child—to calm the nervous pet. In so doing, we convey the power of love one to another, not through the understanding of the mind but through the tenderness of the heart. The gray matter of the brain will one day crumble and decay, but the tenderness of the heart is from everlasting to everlasting and in touching it we have touched immortality. True, the measure of comfort that we pass to another by touch alone is so small that we can hardly call it a healing force. But we need only to connect our human love with the divinely human love of Jesus Christ in order to charge it with power.

It is true that this method does not re-educate the mind. It serves only to relieve the sufferer, to comfort the lonely, to heal the sick. But Jesus was not too high and intellectual to do that very thing. He cleansed the lepers with or without understanding. He healed the maniac without any cooperation at all from that poor sufferer. He took little children in His arms and blessed them whether their parents' theology was right or wrong. These were not His most far-reaching and world-shaking deeds, true. Nor are they ours. The intellectual men whose minds we reach are no doubt more important than the little children whose tears we wipe away through love. But if we are limited to the one method of healing, there will be many sorrowing ones to whom we must harden our hearts. And the more we harden our hearts the more detached we become from humanity. Every spiritual healer knows that he can reach the minds of some but not of all. But there is no one born of woman whose heart he cannot reach through love conveyed simply and humbly as Jesus conveyed it through His physical presence and the touch of His healing hand. Moreover, some people do not know how to teach. But anyone can lay his hand upon a friend in a gesture of love and give himself to the Lord of Hosts to use.

There was an old lady who for many years attended my Bible class. One day she came to me with her face radiant with joy, and told me of her first experiment in healing by faith. She had attended a banquet of the W.C.T.U., of which she had been a faithful and devoted member for some sixty years. Just before dinner she found the speaker of the evening lying on a couch in the ladies' room, faint and ill.

"I knew I could help her," beamed my dear old friend. "But I couldn't have explained it to save my life. So I just said, 'Let me sit here by you and rub your stomach a little bit, and pretty soon you'll feel better.' She smiled, so I pulled up a chair and sat down by her and rubbed her stomach. And as I did I prayed, like you taught us in Bible class. Pretty soon the color came back into her lips and she opened her eyes. 'My, I feel a lot better!' she said. 'I believe I can make that speech, after all.' And dearie, she got up and made it! Afterwards she looked me up and thanked me. 'I don't know who you are and I don't know what you did,' she said, 'but you certainly did help me!' "

I have never seen more joy than shone from the face of this dear lady of eighty-six who had found a new and powerful way of passing on the love of Christ to His children. She still trots around the town to see the lonely and the sick and those who have no helper. Her sweet face is known in homes for the aged and in county institutions. How many her prayers heal no one but the Lord will ever know. But she carries love to some of those who starve to death for lack of love. And her work has eternal value, for love is immortal. Nor does she fail in this life to receive her reward for these cups of living water given to His little ones, for her strength is renewed like the eagle's from year to year.

A friend of mine once went to see her sister who was ill with pneumonia. She took with her a foster-child whom she had instructed in faith.

"Do you think your sister would like for me to put my hands on her chest and say a prayer for her?" asked the little boy.

"I'll ask her," his foster-mother answered.

The sick woman smiled at the bright-faced child and humored him in his desire to pray for her.

"Then you'll have to be very quiet and just think about God," the little boy instructed her.

Obediently the lady closed her eyes.

The child knelt beside her and placed his hands upon her laboring chest. I do not know the words he said, but I know that God was very real to him and he made God very real to the patient, for she recovered in time to come to the table with no effort whatsoever and eat a normal dinner.

Many people will not believe this, I know. Nevertheless it is true, and can be substantiated by two eyewitnesses.

How beautiful upon the mountains are the feet of those who bring good tidings! And how beautiful in the midst of a very cruel world are the hands of those who touch the sufferer with the healing love of Jesus Christ!

There is a high way of contemplation, above the world's sorrow and untouched by the world's pain. But how can we walk that path unless we pass on to those in darkness and in the shadow of death the healing of the immortal love that has lifted us into life? Plato walked the high way, immersed in contemplation of the ideal. But the lonely ones who lived in pain about him were not relieved. Wise men of India for many centuries have trod the lofty peaks of spiritual meditation, developing their psycho-spiritual powers and giving birth to their oversouls. And of all people upon earth their countrymen are the most miserable.

Not by might, nor by power, but by my Spirit, saith the Lord of Hosts.

And His Spirit, being love, humbles Himself and enters into the lowliest and the most sinful, the most ignorant and the most repulsive, through the love of man for man. The greatest works for humanity have been accomplished, not by the learned or philosophical, but by the simple followers of the One who loved everybody. That One knew that His spirit was from everlasting to everlasting. He was nevertheless content to call Himself quite simply the Son of Man. He could have lived always on the highest spiritual plane, seeing only perfection and accomplishing everything by spiritual power. But He did not. He saw sorrowing people, wept for them, loved them and by His love healed them.

"And the Word was made flesh, and dwelt among us."

10

Further Hints On Healing

A very real problem in prayer for others is the initial decision, "Shall I pray for so-and-so? If I decide to take him on, shall I go to see him or shall I just pray from a distance? And if I pray from a distance, shall I tell him that I'm praying for him or shall I not?"

There is a wise old proverb: "If in doubt, don't."

It is not the duty of every Christian to pray for everyone. Our prayers will help some and will not help others, for reasons beyond our understanding or control. Only the Holy Spirit can safely direct our healing power. And if we will listen to the voice of God within, we will be shown for whom to pray. God directs us most joyfully through our own desires. The impulse of love that leads us to the doorway of a friend is the voice of God within, and we need not be afraid to follow it. The impulse of love will also direct our words. The one who goes to a sorrowing friend in the spirit of love will not make the mistake of saying, "I feel that it is my duty to come to see you."

This approach has been forever spoiled by those self-deceived ones who have prefaced their most disagreeable remarks by the ominous phrase, "I feel that it is my duty to tell you this."

Neither will we say, "God told me to come to see you." Maybe He did, but it is often unwise to mention it.

Most people resent the sound of piousness, because they are not very pious themselves. The remainder of the populace resent the sound of piousness because they *are* very pious themselves, and who are you to come telling them things.

If one goes to an acquaintance, one can make it just a social call until the Spirit of God Himself guides the conversation into the paths of faith.

"You're looking fine," the patient may say. "What have you been doing to yourself lately?"

This is a perfect opening.

Or the patient may moan, "I've just about given up."

"Don't do that until you've tried everything!" we can reply.

And when the patient says, "What else is there to try?" we can tell him.

If guided to go to a stranger, we are forced to state the purpose of our call immediately.

"I heard your husband was very sick," we can say. "And I came because I think I can help you."

If we really believe we can help, the stranger will read that confidence within the mind and let us in. Having entered the door, let us not hasten to instruct. Rather, let us quiet ourselves and prepare to listen with the deep comprehension of the one who loves. For love is the pass-key to the mind. Let us love our friends and they will tell us, sometimes intentionally and sometimes unintentionally, the hidden sources of their troubles. Let us look with compassion upon the sorrowful and we ourselves will say the very word of all words that sets free his trust in us.

I once talked with a young Jewish man on the steps of the Academy of Music as we waited for the amphitheatre doors to open. He was a stranger to me but not to his

Father, who loved him greatly and so led the conversation step by step toward the healing of troubled minds.

"Do you think music is on the decline?" the young man asked.

"Oh no!" I replied. "Wars and things like that will be on the decline some day, but music never will."

"Why do you say that wars will be on the decline some day?" he asked.

"Because some day people will find out a more sensible way of accomplishing the purposes of war."

This was enough. He could not rest until he had found out the precise way to which I referred.

"How did you learn these things?" he asked.

"Through the healing of my mind," I told him.

"You don't look as if there had ever been anything the matter with you!"

In order to prove to him that there had been, I mentioned one of the queer mental quirks from which I had suffered. It "happened" to be the very one from which he was suffering.

His eyes filled with tears. "You are a most profound psychiatrist," he said.

But I was not. I was only an ordinary woman who loved him because I saw that he suffered. The love of God does not need a psychiatrist for its conveyor, but can speak through the humble channel of human love and sympathy.

This all-pervasive love directs the words, not only of the one who prays, but also for the sick or troubled one. Often as I sit and listen with keen and loving attention to a tale of woe I pray, "Oh God, please make her say the thing that will give me the key." And the patient goes directly, though often unintentionally, to the inward grief or disharmony that has caused the outer trouble. So the door is open before me. And I enter into that door and make myself a part of that problem, no matter how trivial or sordid it may be. I do not stay on the outside and offer sage advice.

This sounds easy, but they are pitifully few who do it.

"You mustn't think that way!" cries the would-be helper. "You'll never get well while you think that way! My dear, let me tell you—" and she proceeds to hold forth upon her own line—to "sell a bill of goods"—to hand over her own ready-made cure-all. Sometimes it happens to fit the need of the sufferer, and sometimes it does not. In which case the patient listens politely, smiles and says, "Thank you," but does not ask the visitor to come again. And the one who longs to help mourns that the patient has no spiritual understanding.

There is not a living soul who has no spiritual understanding. If the spirit does not respond to us, it may be because we have not sufficient love and sympathy to forget ourselves and look into the being of the one whom we must help.

"You mustn't think like that" may be helpful for a third or fourth visit, but it is almost sure to be wrong for the first.

"I've often felt like that! And isn't it terrible!" is pretty sure to be right.

This is contrary to the very principles of faith that we have been learning, true. But in order to help others we must leave the light and go back into their darkness, so that we can lead them out of their darkness into the light. We need not be depressed by their depression nor take on their symptoms in doing this. Before going to them let us say, "I surround myself with the protection of Almighty God and in the name of Jesus Christ I say that nothing shall get through to hurt me." Thus we go encircled with a shell of protectiveness against either germs or depression. Thus we can enter into the patient's sorrow with a deep serenity, holding the doors of the mind open always for joy. We grieve with the patient because we love him and so his sorrows are ours. Yet we rejoice because we know that God through us is mighty to lead him out of sorrow into joy.

Surrounded thus by faith and joy we need not fear to look into the sorrow of his mind. "I've felt just like that," we can say. "Isn't it awful? Why, I can remember when even the sunshine used to feel black and heavy. Do you know what I mean?"

"I'll say!" the sufferer will reply, light dawning in his eyes. "You've—you've really been like that?"

Upon this we need not fear to go back into our darkest moments and match the patient's feelings pang by pang.

"Oh, that's wonderful!" the patient will sigh. "Most people don't understand at all. They just tell me to snap out of it."

"*Doesn't* that make you mad?" we may say with real sympathy. "Because you can't snap out of it, and when you try, it just makes it worse."

Upon this the troubled one knows that he can talk. And his friend listens, understanding, never contradicting, never correcting, never trying to get across his own ideas . . . only loving the patient and being sorry for him.

"But you're not like that now!" the patient soon notices. "You look great! How did you do it?"

So the door is opened and step by step the one who would help leads him out into the light.

"Don't try to do anything," the friend tells him. "Your mind is too tired. Just let go and let God do it through me."

"I don't know what it's all about, but if you say it works, go ahead," the patient often says. "What do you do?"

"Nothing, except say a prayer for you. I don't want you to kneel because that way you can't relax, and anyway it makes me feel silly. You can just sit there, and if you don't mind I'll stand behind you and put my hands on your head. That way I can forget you and forget me and think about God.''

So the ''difficult'' approach opens as simply and naturally as a flower blooming in the sun. And the power which opens it is the loving understanding of one heart for another.

''I'm afraid of the silliest things,'' a man once said to me. ''There's no use telling you. You wouldn't understand. Nobody does.''

''One of the things I used to be scared of was the telephone,'' I remembered. ''Every time it rang I would break out in a cold sweat.''

''Yeah?'' blurted the patient, surprised. ''Well, I'm afraid of traffic lights! Can you beat that? Gosh! Me! Why, I never used to be afraid of anything, and now I'm scared of traffic lights!''

''I know,'' I laughed. ''And when you see one coming, then you begin to be afraid you'll be afraid, don't you? 'Oh my gosh,' you think, 'I wonder if my mind's going to do like that again?' ''

The gentleman's jaw dropped and he looked at me long and silently.

''Lady,'' he said at last, in the manner of one delivering a formal speech, ''I'll believe anything you say and do anything you tell me to do. Because you are the only person in the world who could ever tell me the way I think inside my own mind.''

Not everyone, true, can meet the psychopathic on his own ground, for not everyone has suffered enough to understand the sufferer from nerves. But many of us have within our own families or among our own friends the sick at heart, the depressed, the melancholic. With them we do not need to seek an approach. We have already approached. We are with them. They are our own. We *must* talk to them. We cannot help it. And whatever we say will either help or harm. Any one of us can help these suffering ones instead of harming them if we will just remember one simple rule: *the sick mind does not respond to reason*.

"My dear, you should snap out of it" to the one suffering from depression is like feeding plum pudding to one suffering from a sick stomach. It is placing an extra burden upon that part of the body that is unable to carry the burden. In these many and most pitiable cases, the mind is sick. If we leave the mind entirely alone perhaps nature will gradually lift it out of depression. But if we goad the mind into making an extra effort we are sure to make it worse.

Jesus did not sit down with those possessed by devils and say, "Now you must make an effort to cast this thing out."

He cast the demon out Himself, asking of the patient no cooperation of any kind, not even faith.

How many lives and minds would be saved if only Christians knew that in dealing with the mentally ill, one does not appeal to their reason!

There was once in China a missionary lady with a depressive tendency. When hardly more than a child I saw it in her face. There was a tightness about her lovely lips and a darkness in her good and patient eyes that hurt me. I once heard her testify at a prayer meeting. She gave thanks that she had been able to rise above a dark and troubled mood. As I heard her something clutched my heart and I looked about the circle of serene faces with a feeling that somebody should do something about poor Mary, and do it quickly! How long it was before her Christian brethren woke up to the fact that this dear, beautiful woman was in mental darkness I do not know. But ten years later I heard that she had committed suicide.

She had told her husband many a time that she was afraid that she would do so. She had even asked him to keep the carving knife hidden.

He had told her that suicide was wrong and that therefore she must not do it. He had called together his fellow-missionaries. They also had spoken to her of her sin and had begged her to pray for forgiveness.

She had found the carving knife one night, but it was not sharp enough. She had hanged herself out of her window by her bedclothes, but she did not hang long enough. She had fallen, but she had not fallen far enough. For three days she lived, while her well-meaning colleagues begged her to confess her sin and ask forgiveness.

They were good people, and they meant well. But they had given her the wrong medicine—they had appealed to her reason.

One appeals to the love of Christ. And one conveys that healing force to the inner being through the law of suggestion.

A girl of sixteen was once brought to me by a schoolmate.

"I'm afraid all the time, day and night," she told me. "I'm afraid of *everything*. Teachers—and people—and things—and just thoughts. I've sat up in a chair now for three nights. I'm afraid to go to bed because when I do the sheets talk to me. And sometimes I say things and don't know what I mean. If something doesn't change inside of me this week, I'm going to kill myself."

Some people say that those who threaten to commit suicide never do so. How anyone can make such a statement in the face of the daily newspapers is hard to see.

"Then we'll have to see that something changes inside of a week," I said.

"How can you do that?"

"I can't. But there's Someone who can."

And I spoke to her of the healing works of Jesus Christ and of His promise that the works that He did we should do also through His power.

"But I don't know anything about Him," the girl objected.

"Well, I do. And when I give an order in His name, it's done. Always."

If I had not been able to speak with absolute confidence, there would have been no use in talking to her at all. Only the sledge-hammer blows of a most powerful faith-suggestion can drive fears from the mind.

"Well, you might as well try it," said the girl.

My faith tottered for a moment. "We'll take away the night-fears first," I said. Perhaps this was childish, but it was better to be childish than to be hypocritical, and I did not feel within myself at that moment the power to take away all her fears at once. "Then come again next week, and we'll take away the day-fears."

I laid my hands upon her head and communed in my mind with the Father of this girl and with His greatest representative among men, my friend Jesus. When I felt His presence without and His authority within, I said loudly and firmly, "In the name of Jesus Christ I direct and order that from this time forth, she shall never again be afraid at night."

"Now that's settled," I told her. "So tonight you can go to bed and you'll sleep all right. If you think you might hear the sheets talking to you—you can fold them up and put them in the closet and sleep between the blankets. But you needn't, for you won't hear them."

The next week she returned.

"How are you?" I asked her.

"Worse than ever in the daytime," she replied.

"How about night?"

"Oh, I'm not scared at *night* any more. That first night I woke up once and saw the chimney that goes through my room. I thought maybe I was going to be scared, so I got up and touched it. And I wasn't scared at all."

So that time we commanded the daytime fears to go away.

For some two years I saw her from time to time. The

fears did not return. Had they been removed by mental suggestion only, they would have returned. But they were removed by the actual inflowing of the forgiveness of Jesus Christ. The mental suggestion was only the key that opened the door to Him, and I was only the one who turned the key.

The depressed mind is the sick mind, always. And the sick mind cannot unlock its own doors to the healing peace of God. But any minister, any friend, any mother, any child, can so unlock the doors of another's mind to Him if the unlocking is done by the power of suggestion and not reason, and if that suggestion is enforced with the strong name of Jesus Christ.

This is not as easy as it sounds. For in order to make the sick mind well the one who prays must believe unfalteringly that it *will* be well. The least shadow of doubt in his mind will blot out some of the sunlight of God's love. If he does not have this sure and radiant faith, he can first learn it by the healing of simple, physical illnesses. For, quite contrary to the common belief, it is much easier to heal the body than to heal the mind.

We do not need to rush forth upon the highways or to mount a soapbox in order to heal the sick. Life itself presents us with plenty of opportunities. We do not need the gift of tongues* nor any ability to instruct, to reason or to argue. We need only a loving heart. Love itself leads us to hold the hand of the sick or to touch the brow. And if it is not suitable or convenient to pray aloud, the prayer can be made in mind alone.

---

*I rejoice greatly in the gift of tongues and in all the gifts of the Spirit. This matter is discussed in a leter book, THE HEALING GIFTS OF THE SPIRIT. But I had done healing for twenty years before I even knew that there was such a thing today as the gift of tongues. The gift of healing was the one I sought, and for the increase of this gift I prayed continually.

I was once asked to see a woman who lay unconscious and very near to death. Her minister's wife escorted me to the house and told her daughter that she wanted me to pray for her.

"But you can't talk to Mamma," whispered the frightened girl.

"I don't need to talk. I'll just stand beside her for about ten minutes and think a prayer in my mind."

"She's—she's not allowed to see anybody," faltered the child.

"She won't see me," I promised cheerfully. "She'll never know I was there. And you needn't tell anybody else I was there, either. Don't be frightened, Honey! Look! If this works, you've got a lot to gain, and if it doesn't, you've nothing to lose."

"O.K.," murmured the girl doubtfully.

So with no further cooperation in faith than this, I stood beside the "dying" woman and laid my hands very lightly upon the bedclothes in the general region of her laboring chest. The touch was too light to rouse her and the spiritual power that passed between us was at too high an intensity and too fine a wave-length for her to perceive.

I never saw her, for the room was dark. I do not even know whether she was informed of my visit or not. But in a few days she was perfectly well.

To what extent this healing added to her understanding or enlightened her spirit I do not know. But I do know that the force which she received was spiritual life. And one cannot receive the life of God without being drawn nearer to God, whether or not he responds to that drawing. However, even if it accomplished nothing whatsoever except to restore her to her children, Jesus healed people just like that because he loved them. And if that was reason enough for Him, it is reason enough for me.

How can an ordinary Christian love a suffering one whom he has never seen?

Christ is the healer. No human being has the power to heal. Christ loves all of us, and sends His love through us to His children according to His will. If we quiet ourselves and let Him speak, we will not go wrong. His love not only directs us to those whom He would have us help, but also directs every word that we say and everything that we do. We know instinctively, for instance, where to lay the soothing hands in prayer. This is usually directly upon the afflicted part, as Jesus laid His hands upon blind eyes and lifeless ears.

A mother whom I knew once laid her hands upon her daughter's ears and said a simple prayer for their healing.

"My!" sighed the little maiden, as a tingling warmth flowed through the mother's hands and soothed her aching ears, "I wish I had two nice, electric hands like yours!"

The mother's was a young and growing faith. Her "nice electric hands" accomplished nothing extraordinary. But at least for a little while, they relieved her daughter's pain. And by doing so, they made God very real to the child.

A natural impulse when God first sends His "electricity" through our hands is to attach too much importance to this outward and visible sign of an inward and spiritual grace. I found myself at one time watching eagerly for the new current of life that flowed through me, feeling disappointed if it did not come and pleased if it did. This distracted my attention from God and focused it on myself, which was wrong. It also caused me unconsciously to command my nerves and try to force a healing vibration from the level of my own mind. Such a vibration can indeed be forced, but it has no healing value whatsoever and only tends to exhaust the one who prays. One must learn therefore to forget oneself entirely and think only of God. If he feels the life of God in a definite flow through his arms and hands, he rejoices in this evidence of a real power, but reminds himself that the tingling of his fingers is not the healing current of God. It is only one of the ways in which he registers a life power that comes from beyond him and is able to function in many different ways. Possibly if his nerves were stronger and more harmonious, he would not register it in this way at all. If he does not feel the presence of God in any physical way, he rejoices that God is not limited to any one way and is at that moment working within him whether he perceives that fact or whether he does not.

The essence of all healing is to become so immersed in the being of God that one forgets himself entirely. And the most successful prayers are those in which the one who prays never thinks of himself at all. He immerses himself first in God and then in his patient. For he will find himself at the end of his prayer listening intently, as it were, to the patient's body. His fingers will report to him the increased effort of the bodily forces. He will feel the swift flow of blood, the twitching of stimulated nerves. In case of a growth, he will often feel an indescribable inner shifting as gentle as a snowball melting in the sun. Often his fingers will report to him concerning the patient's condition. This is not at all strange. He has made a thought-track between his spirit, subconscious mind and body, and the body, the subconscious mind and the spirit of the patient. Neither patient nor doctor may know the exact condition of the patient. But that inner control center, the subconscious mind, is in possession of the facts. And through the telephone-wires of the nerves the subconscious mind of the one who prays often registers these facts. Out of this submerged consciousness the conscious mind picks them up, usually in a vague impression of joy or grief, but sometimes in an actual knowledge of facts that the body has not yet proclaimed to the doctor.

I once prayed for a young man recovering from a ruptured and gangrenous appendix. His recovery, rapid at first, had been retarded and his fever had risen. He was asleep when I removed my hands from the pelvic region and stole out of the room, so I did not speak to him. But I said to the nurse, "He'll be all right," and I opened my mouth to say, "The poison has settled into an abscess, toward the back, probably on the rectum. The doctor will find it soon and remove it and then he'll get well fast."

However, I did not say it. "She'll think I'm crazy," I thought. "And anyway, how do I know that? Maybe I'm wrong."

But the doctors found the abscess on the rectum the next day, treated it, and the young man recovered.

Sometimes the sudden increase of life in the afflicted part causes temporarily an increase of pain, either at that moment or a few hours later. The one who prays should warn the patient of this, so that he will not be alarmed. He should assure the patient that it is a hopeful sign, as indeed it is.

"If the doctor took out that growth it would hurt, wouldn't it?" we can say. "Well, then! God's taking it out by stirring up the healing forces of your own body, so if it hurts some, that's fine. Just bless the pain and put it in His hands, giving thanks that when it has finished what it is doing in there, it will go away."

The blood is the life of the body. We must remember therefore that the blood will tend to rush toward the spot on which we lay our hands. In most cases this is exactly what we wish, but sometimes it is not. In the case of a blood clot, for instance, one should think twice before laying his hands directly upon the affected spot. Perhaps he should place one hand instead between the shoulders where the nerves of all the organs come near the surface of the body, and the other upon the heart. If he wishes to soothe a headache he should also be careful not to increase the flow of blood to the head. He may either place his hands in the position indicated above, which commands the center of the bodily forces, or he may rub the head, drawing his fingers gently from the center of the brow to

the temples and thinking in rhythm "peace—peace—peace."
One should not say a prayer out loud for the sufferer from
headache. That would force the person to think, and so
would increase the flow of blood to the head and make the
headache worse. One need not even command the patient
to have faith; one can simply do for him what he is in too
much pain to do for himself.

I was once directing a pageant upon a certain Christmas
Eve. Most of the characters had made their entrances when
I saw one of the shepherds huddled upon a chair with
closed eyes and labored breath.

"Don't believe I can go on," he moaned. "Got the
most awful headache!"

It is not my usual procedure to rush upon a young man
and rub his brow. But a director will do anything to put on
his play. Therefore I stood behind the young man and
rubbed his forehead, he being too ill to protest.

"This will make it better," I said.

In one minute he sighed with relief and a bit of color
began to come back under his grease-paint. In another
minute he opened his eyes and sat up.

"It feels swell!" he breathed. "There's my cue!" And
he took up his shepherd's crook and made his entrace.

"But is there not a danger in all this loving?" some may
ask.

There is indeed danger in spiritual work, for the tie of
sympathy between us and those for whom we pray is often
very close. There have been "healers" and ministers who
have found themselves so emotionally drawn to certain
patients that in sadness and perplexity they have ceased
praying for healing. But this danger does not come from
too much love. It comes from love drawn from human
sources and not from God.

God is love. Love, then, is of God. Our beings are
charged with love because our beings are charged with God.
The love force within us is the source of all our creativeness.

Through the love of God stepped down into a human voltage in our bodies, our children are born, the children of our flesh and blood and the children of our minds and spirits. That which expresses itself in our marital relations, in our parental affection, in our prayer-life and our business-building and our home-making is the love of God flowing through us. When we do all things in love and to the glory of God, we live in radiance and in power and our lives are balanced and therefore safe. If we cut off love from any department of our lives we injure the tap-root of all love and our lives become either unbalanced or mechanical.

As we live more and more in love with God, the entering in of that high creativity naturally increases within us all the well-springs of love, among them those most high-powered of love-reactions from which our children are born. Many Christians from St. Paul down to certain modern mystics have been frightened by this fact, setting it down to the machinations of Satan, and have endeavored to mortify the deeds of the flesh. Hence the danger. For God is love and love is God and God will not be mortified. Dam up a stream and it will burst its barriers and cause havoc. Cut the tap-root of a plant and it will wither and die. There are well-meaning Christians who feel that in order to be powerful as spiritual workers they must block the love-forces of their natures from their normal channels. This is all very well if they are unmarried and have consecrated themselves to the spiritual life and the sublimation of all the bodily energies into spiritual channels. But if they are married and endeavor to express love "only upon the spiritual plane" they are bound for trouble. At first, true, their spiritual power is increased through this sublimation, because they are forcing all of their creative energy into one channel. But after a while it begins to dwindle because they have shriveled up the very channel through which love flows. Having cut the tap-root of love in their beings, the whole plant withers and dies. Their healing becomes too impersonal, too remote, too far away from the human hearts of men. They may long to help humanity, but humanity withdraws from them. They may feel a high vibration of ecstasy "upon the spiritual plane" that they call "love." But few human beings are wired to receive this rarefied flow of an impersonal goodwill and recognize it as a healing love, and so the hungry hearts of men are still unfilled. And although the one who prays does not know it, something deep and warm and human in his own personality is lost.

Sometimes his inner being protests against this violence done to personality, and the stream of creativity bursts its barriers and results in an unlawful emotional attachment. This danger is not due to too much love to humanity. It is due to too little. And its cure is not less love but more love expressed in every way, in an exuberant and radiant love for husband or wife or child, a love that is not repressed but poured forth joyously and lavishly to the glory of God, who pours forth His love joyously and lavishly in all the teeming processes of creation; in a free outpouring of love for every one of God's children, good or bad, sick or well; in adoration of the world that God has made and in increasing power and success in all creative work.

11

The Healing Of The Emotions

The last chapter brought out a danger in spiritual healing—
the danger of becoming either emotionally sterile or
emotionally unstable. It suggested a defense against this
danger—the rooting and grounding of the emotions in the
supernatural love of Jesus Christ, expressed through the
natural channels of everyday life.

Happy are those who already possess this emotional
stability!

But those who have tried too hard to "live on a spiritual
plane" and have lost their humanness—those whose
emotions, revolting from too much suppression, have back-
fired on them in an unfortunate way—what shall they do?
Shall they obtain emotional release by a method of self-
education, as I have suggested learning other Christian
virtues and graces?

Up to the present time, I have found no way of doing
this. Thought-habits respond to training. Emotions do not.
Acts and words can be directly commanded and controlled.
We can decide what we are going to say and what we are
going to do, but we cannot always decide how we are
going to feel. Our emotions are not under the direct control

of our wills. Only indirectly and in a roundabout manner can we give them the release that they need.

There may be many roundabout ways of securing an emotional release, but for the sake of those who need it I will set down here the most effective way that I have found so far. I found it after much searching and after great need. For I had sent forth the light to so many sick and troubled people that my own light had begun to grow dim. I was like a lamp whose oil was failing. I was like a car driven too long without grease and oil. My thinking developed all kinds of creaks and bumps and rumbles. But so many people depended on me that I did not dare to stop. I forced myself ever onward, putting out greater and greater efforts in hopes of overcoming the ever-increasing strain. For many years I had been a channel through whom others might receive healing. I knew that this healing included forgiveness—that is, the healing of the personality—the changing of the emotional tenor. At this time I realized that I needed forgiveness, and that forgiveness would restore my emotional balance. I had thought a great deal about forgiving others, but I had never thought of being forgiven because I was not in the least conscious of sin.

Indeed, the one danger of the methods in the preceding chapters, if practiced alone—the one danger of forgiving and healing others without a balancing practice in receiving forgiveness—is that it leaves no place for a consciousness of sin. It closes our eyes to those lingering faults of our human nature that lie deep in the subconscious. It leads directly toward the sin of spiritual pride that is the downfall of most spiritual leaders. However, while I did not know that I needed forgiveness I knew very well that I needed *something*. "Oh Lord, I've just got to have more power!" I prayed. "Show me a way to get it!"

And He showed me, in a way that seemed strange indeed to me at first, simply because it was so ordinary—so old—so absolutely fundamental!

Through the advice of a friend, I tried the confessional. "The confessional is the church's way of passing on power," she told me. And I retranslated these words to mean "The confessional is the church's way of giving a healing treatment."

I was astonished beyond measure. "If that is so, why have I lived all these years without being told?" I demanded. "Why have I been allowed to think that the confessional was only an escape for neurotics or a desperate measure for criminals?"

To this question the friend had no answer.

"Just the same, it is so," she said. "The confessional sets free in you the power of God through the forgiveness of Jesus Christ. It releases power in the way that is the most simple and wholesome and human. If you try and get that power all by yourself, you are apt to overstrain your spiritual energies. The only way you can go on and on getting it alone is to close your eyes to humanity and try and live on a spiritual plane. That method isn't new. It has been tried in the middle ages and given up. It is good as far as it goes, but it doesn't go far enough. And unless one combines it with the sacramental method, it tends to spiritual dryness and exhaustion. Some people can overcome that and go on, living more and more on a spiritual plane. But that separates them from other people. They deny their humanity instead of redeeming it, and so they get farther and farther away from ordinary human beings. They get cold and remote. They build a wall around themselves so that people cannot get near them."

All of this I recognized. It had all happened to me. But I still did not understand the need of the confessional.

"I know that if you believe in Jesus Christ He forgives your sins," I puzzled. "I've known that all my life. Then why do I need to go to any other person and confess my sins so as to be forgiven?"

"Try it and you will find out," said my adviser.

"Well, all right," I replied. "I'll try anything once. After all, that's the way I've found out everything else—by trying it. What do I do?"

Upon this my new friend gave me careful and particular instructions which I shall set down precisely as I received them. I do so, not because everyone who reads this book will rush to the confessional. Having been brought up strictly in the Presbyterian fold I know full well how impossible this would be for many people. But the principles worked out in the following method are universal. They are the best ways that I know for obtaining an emotional balance. And if one is unable to use them in the form of the confessional because one cannot find a minister who believes in it, they can be adapted and used in other forms.

The suggested method for that form of soul-searching that the Bible calls repentance is as follows. Choose the same time and the same place every day for an act of preparation for confession. Relax and lift the mind into the presence of God, and do so with a pencil and paper in the hand. Then divide one's life into seven periods.

Throw the mind back, on the first day, into the nearest period. Ask the Holy Spirit of God to bring into the remembrance any unforgiven sins (or any uncomfortable memories, as we would probably call them) from these years that still linger in the subconsciousness. Write down these sins as they come to mind. Write them down simply, briefly, without using names or mentioning circumstances or any kind of alibis. Having done this, set aside the paper and forget the whole matter until the next day.

On the next day at the same time and the same place take the second period of one's life and do the same thing. And so on through the seven days.

The little things that come to mind may seem childish, and so they are. But the method is nevertheless right. For why would childish things linger just below the level of consciousness all these years unless there were in them some unhealed hurt—some unforgiven sin? They are like splinters in the hand. The thing may be invisible, but as long as it is there it festers a bit. So the splinters of uncomfortable memories (unforgiven sins) fester in the subconsciousness and throw out into the conscious mind various symptoms of fears, nervous tensions, etc., of whose cause we are completely unaware.

Upon the last of these days, my adviser told me, it might be well to make a retreat of twenty-four hours so as to put my mind entirely upon this thing. She also advised me to go to a priest whom I did not know.

So I made a first confession, very uncomfortably, with the shades of my Scotch Presbyterian ancestors peering around the corners. I followed the strict cut-and-dried form of the church. I read the opening prayer in which I stated that I was guilty of certain sins, by my fault, my own fault, my own grievous fault. I thus had no chance to call these things errors rather than sins as I would undoubtedly have called them otherwise. It was not possible to use the words "negative thought-habits" or "unfortunate decisions" or "nervous tendencies." Neither was it possible to make an excuse or alibi of any kind. There was no dotted line in the form of confession set before me on the prayer-desk for any "But he did so-and-so, or she said so-and-so, or life treated me after this or that fashion." I was forced to look squarely upon all my failings, to call them sins and to accept full responsibility for the same. Others may have sinned ten times more than I concerning a certain thing. That made no difference. I was responsible in the sight of God for my own sin, not for that of anyone else. If someone had gossiped about me, lied about me, slandered my name and ruined my life it was nevertheless my duty to confess only to the sin of resentment toward him.

Thus I was forced by an ancient, simple, cut-and-dried

method to a self-searching and a straight-thinking that was as uncomfortable and as cleansing as a strong cathartic.

Having read through my list, without comment, I then ended with the printed prayer on the desk before me in which I said I was truly sorry for these and all my other sins that I could not at the time remember and that I intended to do better.

Whereupon the priest made one statement and only one. He said, "Although so few people know it, the church through Jesus Christ really does have the power and authority to forgive sins. Therefore I am sure that these your sins will be forgiven." He then pronounced the absolution, as I had heard the priest pronounce it many a time in the communion service, and I rose and went out, still without comment.

This was done by an act of will and of will only. There was no emotion connected with it except a feeling of distinct discomfort. To kneel in the presence of another person, even though I knelt to the cross and not to him, was not a pleasant experience. There was not even in my mind a feeling of faith or of expectancy. Indeed, my adviser had made it very plain that I must not expect any feeling of joy or of release because the power of God worked in varying ways and the emotions were not a correct indicator of the power of its working. So I arose and went out feeling stiff and cold both in my knees and in my mind.

But I had hardly gone out of the place before I was flooded from head to foot with the most overwhelming vibrations. I felt a high ecstasy of spirit such as I had felt before when very spiritual people had prayed for me. I felt a deep inner burning which I had felt when receiving a "healing treatment" from someone who had the faith to set free the healing power of God in prayer. I knew by the inner warmth and tingling that my nerves and glands were being healed of their overstrain and weakness. And indeed a healing process did begin in me at that time. But in addition to these manifestations of the grace of God through the forgiveness of Jesus Christ I felt something else that I cannot put into words. I can only say that I felt for the first time that Jesus loved me. Something touched my heart. A stream of tenderness was released within me. And I knew that this was the forgiveness of Jesus Christ—His life, given for me.

Jesus saw that we need not only His teachings but also His life. He tried saving people by His teachings alone and it did not work. His principles were right, but they were continually short-circuited by the forces of evil in this world. God's love was blacked out from man by the negative thought-vibration of this sinful and suffering world. The sins of man had created a thunder-cloud, as it were, that shut out the free shining of God's love. So our Lord in the garden of Gethsemane undertook the great work that we call the atonement—the at-one-ment which reunited man with God. He literally lowered His thought-vibrations to the thought-vibrations of humanity and received unto Himself man's thoughts of sin and sickness, pain and death. And as He was the Son of God and therefore able to transcend time, He took unto Himself all of the sinful thought-vibrations of all humanity, past, present and future.

For this also He died. Having received our sins into Himself by an effort so great that it literally broke His heart, as the account of the crucifixion shows, He then sent out to us the love of God in a rush of power that broke down the dam of man's hate. He did this upon the cross, so that His death might be a matter of state record, testified to beyond any doubt. But His death, taking place in three hours, was not caused by the cross. It was caused by the weight of man's sins upon a heart that had known no sin. We are fond of blaming His death upon those people whom He chose as His brothers and His friends, His apostles and His martyrs—the Jews. We would do better to consider those sins of our own that formed part of the burden that He bore.

Having borne our sins He turned them into holiness, and sent them forth into the air again cleansed and purified. Having received man's hate He turned it into love and directed it out into the world again. So He cleansed the thought-vibrations that surround this globe as a purifying plant cleanses our drinking water, taking it in dirty, throwing it up into the sunlight and sending it forth clean. So He removed the thunder-cloud of man's hate and released the clear shining of God's love.

Thus He set flowing a stream of life within life, like the Gulf Stream within the ocean or like the main current within a river. This does not contradict anything about the universal love of a God who sends His rain on the just and on the unjust. It only adds something to it. It adds a specific and personal current of love to that love which is universal. It adds love to love—power to power—life to life.

This costly gift has staggered the imagination of the wise for two thousand years and has been received with simplicity by the childlike.

If we are too wise to receive it, that is no reason why we should abandon any help we may have gained from the universal love of the God of all men. A magnifying glass can provide for us a concentrated sunlight that can set on fire a piece of paper placed beneath it. But if we have no magnifying glass or if we do not care to experiment with so great an energy, that is no reason why we should stay out of the sunlight. Some who read this book may not be able to accept this chapter. If so, they would be wise to lay it on the table, as it were, and proceed with their methods of self-help until such time as they need a deeper power. Or if that time never comes, they would still be wise to absorb as much of the universal life of God as He graciously sets free for them.

If I were to place a piece of paper beneath a strong magnifying glass in the sunlight and see it catch on fire, I might not understand the reason for the phenomenon, but nevertheless seeing it I would believe that it was so.

Through the confessional my heart caught on fire. Its dullness and boredom was burned away, its coldness was turned to warmth, its pride was melted into humility. From that time forth I owed all things to all men, for the sake of Him who loved me and gave Himself for me. But at first I did not understand the reasons for this marvelous grace of God. Why, I thought, was it necessary for me to have a mediator of the forgiveness of God in order to receive this grace? Why had I not been able by myself to repent of my sins and to receive full forgiveness? I had always believed in the forgiveness of sins through Jesus Christ. Then why had it not worked for me by my own efforts?

In the same way I had wondered years ago why healing had not come to my baby through my own prayers.

I could give many reasons for this. I could point out the difficulty of seeing our own sins, much greater than the difficulty of seeing our own illnesses. I could explain the value of two minds working together, the one to accomplish an act of repentance, the other to send forth the word of power, the assurance of forgiveness. But the words of the Bible are so absolutely clear and plain on this subject that my own seem trivial beside them. In John 20:22,23, we read, "Receive ye the Holy Ghost; whose soever sins ye remit, they are remitted unto them; and whose soever sins ye retain, they are retained." In James 5:16 this direction is given, "Confess your faults one to another, and pray one for another, that ye may be healed." And in St. John's first epistle we have this fact presented again and again with brilliant clarity by the disciple who best understood the mind of the Master. "The blood of Jesus Christ His Son cleanseth us from all sin. If we say that we have no sin, we deceive ourselves, and the truth is not in us. If we confess our sins, He is faithful and just to forgive us our sins and to cleanse us from all unrighteousness. If we say that we have not sinned, we make Him a liar, and His word is not in us.''

No words of mine could be so straight and so definite as *that*.

However, I had always known this. I had been brought up in the knowledge that the blood of Jesus Christ cleansed from all sin, and had never doubted it for a moment. Yet I was not released from that bondage until I tried the confessional and since then my release has come step by step as I have seen more and more clearly my need of forgiveness.

Merely believing that God has the power to cure diseases does not cure the disease. I had found out by experience that one needed to be more specific and definite than this. In order to be a channel for God's healing to another I had to believe that God had the power and the will to heal that specific disease of that specific person through me, at that time. In the same way I found out by experience that just believing in Jesus Christ and His power to forgive sins does not make one into a perfect person. One needs to be more specific and more definite than that. One needs first to see one's own faults clearly, and secondly, to believe that God is able to remove those faults then and there, and to create in one precisely the opposite virtues. If one can and does do this without the aid of priest or spiritual friend, psychiatrist or medical adviser, well and good. I know a few people who can, and do. But they are saints and this is a book for ordinary little people. Very few of us ordinary people do this by our own efforts. It is comforting to know that if we have not and cannot do it for ourselves there is still a way open to us, even though it is a way that seems difficult at first.

It seems, as a matter of fact, more difficult than it is. It is like jumping into cold water. After the plunge, it is all right! And the hardness of that first plunge is due quite simply to one specific sin—pride. We who have sought Him with our minds do not like to fall upon our knees and to receive Him in our hearts. It flatters our intellects to think that we can learn and practice what He taught. It does not flatter us to think that we can receive His life through a humble acceptance of His forgiveness. Yet that forgiveness is His very life given for us—His perfect love given for our feeble and imperfect love, His strength for our weakness, His health for our illness, His life for our death. For the current of His forgiveness sweeps through the shallows of this world toward the deep waters of everlasting life.

12

The Healing Power Of Forgiveness

Not every Christian belongs or would care to belong to a church that makes use of the confessional.

Fortunately, the confessional is not the only way of receiving the forgiveness of Jesus Christ. For instance, I once talked to a discouraged young man in an army hospital. His back was broken and apparently his spirit was broken, too, for I found him very big-eyed and sad in a psychopathic ward. I tried to tell him of the Life that could mend his broken back.

"You know, doctors tell you that nature makes you well," I said. "Well, what is nature? It's God's life in you, isn't it?"

"I guess so," he murmured dubiously.

And I tried to explain to him how to renew a sort of spiritual blood transfusion in his body.

"But I think that's contrary to my religion," he objected. "I'm a Roman Catholic."

"Then it's not contrary to your religion at all!" I replied. "It's just exactly what your church teaches you! Don't they teach you that our Lord sends His real life into the elements of the blessed sacrament?"

"Yes," he murmured, brightening.

"Well, if that real presence is His body and blood, doesn't it include His bones? And can't you receive it in your backbone?"

"Why—sure! I hadn't thought of that, but—sure!"

"Then I'll pray for you to receive it in just that way. And I'll ask my friends the Sisters to pray for you every morning at the Mass. And that Life will go from the Mass right through their prayers into your spine. You'll see!"

So I left him very happy. And to the sacramental method I added, unknown to him, my own method. I was very sure that he would receive life through the Mass, because he believed that he would. But I also practiced seeing his spine well and perfect and shining with that Life.

Six weeks later I looked for the depressed young man in his bed and did not find him. But I heard his voice upraised in merriment so I pursued him into the main ward. There he was, mopping the floor, cast and all, and shouting at the top of his lungs to everybody. He put down the mop when he saw me and led me into the ward kitchen, where he offered me a glass of milk, as if he were the Grey Lady and I were the wounded soldier.

"These here doctors, they burn me up," he stated. "I didn't ask to come into this hospital! They pick me off a battlefield, see, and carry me into a hospital and say I have a broken back. And there I've been ever since, one hospital after another. *Now* what do they say? They take another X-ray, see, and they say 'Well, did you break your back or didn't you?' Gosh! Do they burn me up!"

"Don't you remember that we asked the body of our Lord to go into your back and mend it?"

"Yep."

"Well, He did, that's all. And you can't blame the doctors for not understanding that."

Some of us are able to receive forgiveness and its resultant healing through that powerful combination, the confessional followed by the communion service. Some of us can make use of the communion service and not of the confessional. Some of us belong to a church that makes little or no use of either. But the principles that underlie these sacramental methods can be re-translated to meet the needs of everyone.

I worked out a practical method, which can with slight modifications be used by anyone. Those of us who use this method try from Sunday morning to Friday to live as heirs of God's power, doing His works and thinking His thoughts. Then on Friday or Saturday, we leave the heights and come down into the depths of our beings. We ask God's Spirit to come into us and guide our memory. Then we look back over the week and write down every sin that comes into our minds.

This is not so difficult as one would think. For God is very merciful and He guides us in what we remember. He does not show us at one time all the faults and failings in our subconsciousness. He shows us only those wrong deeds or unworthy thoughts that He wants us at that time to correct.

Having seen our faults, we then ask Him what He wants us to do about them. The Bible tells us if we have defrauded any man to restore it four-fold. So the least we can do if we have short-changed anyone or cheated anyone (either in physical or in spiritual matters) is to restore it. If we have cheated anyone or underpaid anyone, we should make it up to them in cash. If we have lied, we should apologize for the lie and correct it. If we have spoken rudely or unkindly to anyone, we should say that we are sorry.

"But that is ridiculous," we are apt to think. "Those are such trifling faults!"

Yes, and for that very reason they keep God out. For He is not trifling. He is not petty. And every petty sin keeps out some of His love. For it comes back to one simple fact:

sin separates us from God. In fact sin *is* separation from God. And we must then seek His forgiveness, set free through Jesus Christ, to set us free from these sins.

It is like seeing in our minds a beautiful picture and painting it and then examining it when the glow of inspiration has faded out in order to see its mistakes and correct them. First we create, then we look at the created thing to see if it is good, then we correct those things that can be improved.

Even God checked up on His creative work at regular intervals! "And God saw every thing that He had made, and behold, it was very good."

There will be some things on our list that we cannot correct by our own efforts. Gossip once started cannot be stopped. Lost opportunities for kindness and helpfulness cannot be regained. Hate or wrongly directed love cannot be atoned for by apology. There is nothing we can do then to take out of our minds the sting of these things. But there is One who can do it for us. And He is willing to do so on one condition, which is that we accomplish an act of repentance for them.

Then let us on this one day learn to repent. It begins with being sorry for our sins, but it ends with joy, because it ends with a changed life. So let us come to Him, literally upon our knees, and think of His great act of self-giving. Let us tell Him how unworthy we are of such great love and how grateful we are for it. Let us tell Him also that we do not really understand the need for Calvary, and ask Him to help us understand it. We cannot fully comprehend the atonement, but we do know that He loved us. Let us ask Him then to send this love into the very depth of our subconscious minds and there wipe out the thought-impressions of our sins.

Then let us go to church on Sunday and give thanks to Him, publicly and in cooperation with our fellowmen, for the healing and cleansing power of His love. If we are not accustomed to going to church or if we do not admire the minister, then our going will be all the more effective. It will be an act of real courtesy that we do for Him in return for His great courtesy to us.

To end this act of repentance and of the acceptance of forgiveness at a definite time, such as the time of church-going, is a very important thing. If we do not do so we may fall into a permanent habit of self-condemnation, and nothing can be more unhealthy than that.

Whether one has access to the confessional or not, one can still find forgiveness in the church service. One can receive His forgiveness in silent prayer and express one's gratitude for it aloud in hymns.

And if one wants to make doubly sure that he will really receive the forgiveness of Jesus Christ in this way, he can ask a spiritual friend to pray for it to happen.

There was a young man for whom I had prayed many times. He had been brought back from the doors of death by prayers for healing. And in due time the prayers for healing began in him a work of forgiveness.

"Come, quick!" cried his wife, running into my house. "Danny feels terrible!"

"What's the matter? Another attack?"

"No. It isn't that. I don't know what it is, but he feels terrible!"

I found Danny in tears. "It's those thoughts," he said. "You don't know what a bad guy I've been. And now when I try to pray, those awful thoughts just go around and around in my head and I can't stop them. I think I'm going nuts!"

I told him that Jesus Christ could stop those thoughts and put good thoughts in his mind instead. That was, I told him, the forgiveness of sins. And we would pray for it together just as we had prayed together for healing. So I put my hands on his head, the better to transfer the power that forgives and heals, and prayed for the love of Christ to reach him through me. In the name of Jesus Christ I commanded those thoughts to stop. Finally I stated through faith in the redemption of Jesus Christ that I knew that his sins were forgiven. Thus Danny made a confession and I pronounced the absolution though neither one of us had the least idea what we were doing.

It worked. But as weeks passed the thoughts gradually crept back into his mind again. This time I tried a different method. I suggested that he read over the communion service very carefully and that he do just what the prayer book said to do, and that he go to church on Sunday morning especially to receive the complete forgiveness of his sins. And I told him that I would be there praying for him at that time. We kept this assignment with the Lord. He returned from the altar bathed in tears but a new man, and in spite of many ups and downs he has been a new man ever since.

One more question occurs to me in regard to this matter of confession and repentance. If it worked such wonders with me, why does it not work with equal power for everyone? Why does not everyone who goes to the confessional receive there a healing of body as well as of soul? Why does not every Christian who repents on his knees show forth the results in a life of power?

For the same reason that every Christian who believes in God does not receive healing—lack of faith. They believe that Jesus Christ can forgive sins, yes. But to believe that He can heal them of a hot temper so that they will be gentle in disposition—to believe that He can change their hate of husband or wife into love—to believe that He can remove from them the craving for drink—this is a different matter.

Not only do most people lack this faith, but they lack the technique for learning it. They do not know how to rise from an attitude of repentance into an attitude of the joyful acceptance of forgiveness. They remain in a state of self-condemnation—a most unhealthy attitude.

The swing-up into joy and power is as important as the swing-down into repentance. To announce oneself a miserable sinner once a Sunday is excellent if one recognizes oneself as a joyful saint immediately afterwards and strives throughout the week to do the work of the Lord. It is very difficult to set free the healing power of God in another while in a state of repentance for one's own sins. The mind turned in on itself cannot sufficiently vision wholeness and light in the patient. I have found only one way of praying for another with real power while accomplishing an act of repentance. This is the ancient method of reparation wherein one makes available the sacrificial love of Christ for another by assuming his sins and doing penance for them. But while powerful, this is a costly and difficult method and one beset with many dangers. Moreover the time element alone forbids it being generally used.*

One must be very careful in using these two methods of prayer (the way of affirmation and power, and the way of repentance and humility) to make a clean swing back and forth from one to the other. It is quite impossible to think both ways at the same time and we are not intended to do so. He who knew the mind of man provided two ways as a balance for each other.

There was a man who said that he had to give up being a Christian Scientist because he got tired of being "so damn happy" the whole time. The more intensely we think after one pattern the more surely we get tired of it; the more definitely we need to drop it now and then and think after a different pattern. Our minds are made that way. Even our bodies are made that way. We do not sleep

_____

*This method of healing is both taught and illustrated in my novel, LOST SHEPHERD.

all the time, and we do not thirst all the time. Even nature does not demonstrate continually after one pattern. There is summer and winter, day and night, full moon and dark of the moon, high tide and low tide, wind and calm. There is the swing of the sun and moon in their courses and of the planets and of all the stars. For the law of rhythm, of balance, holds throughout the universe.

Blessed is he, therefore, who undergoes periods of hungering and thirsting after righteousness, and rejoices at other times in being filled.

13

Intercession: Healing From A Distance

After my confession experience, I tried immediately to turn the tide of life that I felt within me into the healing of others. It did not occur to me to receive the forgiveness of Jesus Christ for myself alone. To accept such a gift only to store it away in the bank of heaven that I might cash in on it after death would surely be to lose it. "He that saveth his life shall lose it."

It seemed to me, however, that the attitude of repentance made prayers for others more difficult. I had been thinking as a miserable sinner and who was I to claim and use the power of God? Then I realized that to refuse to claim the power of His forgiveness was as great a sin as to neglect to ask for it. I had asked Him to forgive my sin and reinstate me as His child. If I did not believe that He had done this, was I not denying Him again?

As soon as I had seen this clearly, I was able to send forth once more those thoughts of sinlessness that are the thoughts of power. And I was able to think them much more effectively, because the foundation beneath them was deepened and strengthened. Moreover I found a great new source of strength in prayer—the real, vivid, human feeling of the loving presence of Jesus Himself, working in me and through me.

For instance I once found a young man in an army hospital suffering intensely from headache.

"When I was a little girl I used to rub my mother's head and the headaches would get well," I said. "Would you let me try to help you?"

"Couldn't help this headache," he smiled. "I was hit by a truck."

"It won't hurt to try," I pleaded, and the boy, too ill to resist me, smiled and yielded.

I imagined Jesus there beside me and talked to Him. "Here you are and here's your child," I said inwardly. "Please lay your own hands on him and do whatever you want to do through me."

There was no question in my mind about what He wanted to do. Did His will ever change? Did His love ever waver?

"That's funny," he said presently, opening his eyes. "It's much better. What were you doing?"

"I was praying."

He smiled. "I'm Jewish," he said. "But I believe in prayer, too."

"I'm glad you're Jewish," I replied.

"Why?"

"Because I'm Christian, and I don't think we have been very nice to your people. So I'm glad of any chance to help a little bit."

Some may wonder whether it is right to pray in the name of Christ and by the power of Christ for one who might not be willing to accept Christ. But after all, was it not that way when He was on earth? Did the nine lepers accept Him as Saviour? Did the lame and halt and blind who came to Him understand the theology of a redemptive work yet to be accomplished? Indeed no! They saw a light through the darkness of this world—that was all. And if any of His brethren, the Jews, can see that light through me, then I am grateful. They will need to see the light of love through many a Christian before they will be likely to receive the Lord of love.

I have come to see healing and forgiveness and world-prayer as three aspects of the same thing—the channeling of the redemptive love of Jesus Christ into the world. And through tapping the ever-flowing stream of His forgiveness I have somehow reached a deeper and more human level of prayer-power. I am not limited to healing through lifting the understanding of the patient into the light of God's love. God in His mercy can also work through me according to a deeper law—the law of the forgiveness of sins through the life of Jesus Christ, given for us.

This law will work at a distance as well as in the presence of the sick person. But the method of intercession is much more difficult than healing at the bedside of the sick. Perhaps that is why Jesus so seldom used it. He nearly always went to see the one whom He would heal. When one prays with a sick person he has the cooperation of the patient's agreeing mind and of his relaxed and attentive body. He has also the full use of all his own energies, spiritual, mental and physical. When he sends the healing power of God from a distance, he must find his way into the patient's subconsciousness through all the conflicting thought-vibrations of this troubled world, and he is thrown entirely upon his spiritual energy in doing so, since he does not have access to the patient's mind or body.

The first step in intercessory prayer is to find out the will of God—God's assignment to that individual for prayer. For God divides His children into bundles, as Thomas Kelly says, and gives a bundle to each of us lest we be burdened overmuch. He gives us the desire to pray for those who are ours. We feel for them a "concern," as the Friends call it; an eager and joyful desire to pray for them and to help ourselves, holding each suggested person up before the Lord and seeking for His guidance concerning our duty toward that person.

Sometimes He fills our hearts with love for the patient, so that we long to see him. If this be the case, let us go to him gladly, knowing that the door is open.

Sometimes, while willing to go to see the sufferer, we feel no urge to do so. If that be the case, let us pray where we are and feel our way across the miles in prayer.

I was once asked to pray for a little boy whose head had been crushed by a bus and who had been in a coma for two weeks. I therefore went into the chapel, stilled myself before the Lord and asked His instructions concerning this matter. The answer was almost as clear as a voice within my mind: "Pray for him now, from this place, and he will recover."

I prayed, and felt after the prayer that sense of peace and of release that means that the prayer-work is finished. So I knew that the child had recovered.

It was not necessary for me to see him, because the direct contact was being made by other hands than mine. Two Roman Catholic Sisters were at that very moment in prayer with him, as they had been many a time before. They did not know that the great Stage-Manager had brought me into the wings, nor did I know that they stood on stage before Him and before the child. But with that unconscious cooperation His will was done. The child opened his eyes and asked for his supper, and was well from that time on. So it is in the great world of prayer, for we are all one in Christ Jesus.

Sometimes when we hold the patient up before the Lord, we find that we cannot pray for him with joy. We feel a heaviness as we think of him—a coldness, a lassitude, a darkness. This is clearly an indication that we are not to pray for the patient's recovery at all. As we become skilled in prayer, we dare go one step further, to ask, "Lord, will he recover?" and then face the answer. The answer is like a door closed in the face, not with the harsh bang of unbelief but with the gentle finality of a loving hand. It is like an inner voice that whispers, "No."

God's perfect will for this His child is life, as it is always life. But His infinite wisdom knows that the sum of the skill of the doctors, the faith of the patient and my own spiritual development is such that in this life His will is not to be completed. In other words, the kingdom of Heaven has not yet fully come. Our earthly mansions are not yet completely wired for the flow of heavenly electricity. And until we have helped the great Electrician complete His work, we must be content with what light we have.

In such a case as this the one who prays can but ask again for guidance. Sometimes when he does so, the case will slip out of his mind as definitely closed as a closed book. Thus he knows that it is not his "bundle."

At other times he will find that he cannot forget; that his love and sympathy draw him to the one in trouble. In that case he can do nothing else but go and pray with him, making his prayers for life big enough and loving enough to include all Life. The patient has asked him to go a mile with him, and he must go two miles, up to the gates of the great Life that men call death. The last mile is a very weary mile. But all along the way there is the joy of holding one we love above suffering and pain and of freeing a spirit very gently from the ties of the flesh.

I first went the second mile with a friend whose body was full of cancer. We never spoke of death, only of Life. And so gentle was her passing into that Life that she knew no pain. In fact, five days before she died I found her sitting in her kitchen peeling asparagus. Her last words to me, simple, homely words, spoken in dying, were these: "Agnes, I feel fine, only I can't breathe very well. As soon as I get over this funny feeling in my chest, I'm going to be all right." And so she was, for she slipped into heaven as gently as a child going to sleep. When she got over that funny feeling in her chest she was in a new and radiant life, and she was indeed all right.

"Just let go now," I said to her when her spirit was departing. "And the same Power that has gone with you all the way will help you over the edge. It will be as easy as breathing. . . ."

Her conscious mind was no longer with me, but her spirit heard me and smiled, for there was a peace upon her face as she departed.

So the first step in intercessory prayer is to quiet ourselves before God and with His guidance to choose our path, fearing not to follow it wherever it may lead.

The second step is to contact the power that heals and fill ourselves full of it. Love is the healer. The One who loved us and gave Himself for us is the One who heals.

We may try to heal from the level of our own minds and wills and we may for a time succeed, but we will exhaust our nervous energy in doing so. We may rise a step higher and heal by the contemplation of the ideal, by immersing ourselves so completely in the spiritual realities of health and joy and peace that we see nothing else. This is beautiful and good. As a step toward God, it is perfect. But as a final achievement it is not perfect, for if we live only as spiritual beings we leave the world too far behind. And if we concentrate our vision upon God as truth, as light, as creativity, and think of the Christ only as the spirit of God that abides in all of us and of Jesus only as the first demonstrator of that spirit, we tend to become remote—vague—far away from man. We may feel a glory within us—a spiritual glory—but others do not see it, and we become separated from our fellowmen.

There is only one in all the world who dwelt perfectly in God and yet remained firmly in the flesh, enduring it until the very end: the man Jesus Christ. He ever lives and makes intercession for us. He is, in other words, always attuned to our prayers, always sending out to us the infinite and eternal light of God clothed in the thought-vibration of humanity. In order to fill ourselves with the power of God, then, let us fill our spirits and minds and hearts with Him.

In order to fill ourselves with His whole being, let us think of Him, imagining His presence, seeing Him with the eyes of the mind, trying to love Him with the heart. Let us beseech Him to come and dwell within us. Let us ask Him to enter into our spirits and fill us with His own consciousness of the fatherhood of God; to enter into our minds and think within us His own thoughts; to enter into our hearts and feel through us His own love, directing it to those who need it most; to enter into our bodies and build them up according to the pattern of His perfect holiness, making us more and more fit channels for the inflow and outflow of His life.

Above all if we really want to love Him and feel His love for us, let us kneel before His cross, dare to contemplate His sufferings thereon and thank Him for His inestimable gift to us. Let us then thank Him for the great gift of his own life. Let us dwell upon Him and immerse ourselves in Him until the reality of His being fills us and floods us with power. As we do this, our healings become free and easy and spontaneous, for we know that we are doing nothing at all. The great friend of man is doing His own works through us.

Perceiving this with an inner certainty we know that there is no death. There is now no condemnation to those who are in Christ Jesus. There being no condemnation, there can be no severance of power, and that stream of creativity that flowed through Jesus Christ, through Peter and James and John, through Paul and Francis of Assisi and bishops and priests and the praying souls of all ages, is flowing through our small, attentive selves and making a stream of power that nothing can withstand.

As we pray for His indwelling, we become aware of an inrush of power. Some of us feel an actual current of life entering into the center of the body and rising through the spine. So forceful is this vibration or stream of life that we are forced to keep the spine erect and the breathing light and even. For a little time we cannot speak. We are so filled with the fullness of Christ that there is within no room for words.

Being so filled with His life, we must needs send it forth. So the third step of intercessory prayer is the connecting of the healing force with the one who needs healing. Having turned our thoughts up toward God, we now turn them down toward man. And the success of our prayer depends as much on the depth of our love to man as on the height of our love to God.

Some of those in convents and monasteries pray with continual fervor and with great benefit to themselves and to the world, but with little or no actual healing results to the sick and sorrowing who ask their prayers. They have learned to rise into God, but they have not learned to sink again into man. They reach a high state of religious contemplation and there they stay. But their prayers for healing can be more effective as they learn how to project the power of God into the being of man.

They are like a doctor who has made up a powerful prescription but has not given it to his patient. Thus they follow Jesus part of the way, but not all of the way. He went onto the mountain-top to pray. But He did not stay upon the mountain-top. He came down once more into the woes of man and healed them, every one.

New doors are now opening for the holy and beloved ones in religious communities. More and more of them are receiving the power of the Holy Spirit and doing among men the works of prayer and healing that Jesus did. Also they are learning when they pray to "see the person well," and thus to accept the healing by faith, that it should be made perfect.

For a long time I did not know how to give the prescription to the patient from a distance. How could I reach across the miles in prayer? Finding no answer to this question in my own church, I sought the answer elsewhere. I inquired of a lady minister who through her open-mindedness had found a practical application of the eternal verity of God that my own church had insufficiently grasped.

"How do you do it?" I asked her. "I can help them when I'm with them, but my prayers from a distance don't seem to result in healing at all."

"Oh my dear, you're seeing them sick," cried the beautiful old minister.

"What do you mean?" I asked, puzzled. "I'm not seeing them at all, I'm just thinking of them. And, of course, they're sick, or I wouldn't be praying for them."

"Yes, you are seeing them," she replied patiently. "When you think of someone, you always see the person in your mind. If you really believe he's going to be well, you see him well. If he pops into your mind as your eyes saw him last, or as your friend tells you he is, all moans and groans and fever, that shows that your subconscious mind does not really believe he's going to be well. And so you only fasten the illness on him. When you pray for someone, you must learn to see him *well*."

And the voice within me said, "That's right."

We pray not only with the conscious mind. Nine-tenths of the thinking is in the subconsciousness, and the spirit uses the path of the subconscious in sending forth the power of prayer. Therefore if the subconsciousness retains the picture of the person sick, the spirit can send at best only a divided message, suggesting life and death, health and illness at the same time.

From that time forth I set myself to learn to "see them well." This required mental training. I would exercise my visual faculty, that part of the creative imagination that is most like God. I would create in my mind a definite and detailed picture of each person for whom I prayed, seeing the whole body radiant and free and well, with light in the eyes and color in the cheeks and a swinging rhythm in the walk. I would raise him in my mind from a hospital bed and see him walking, running, leaping. By an act of will I would hold this picture in my mind until it outshone the picture last suggested to me by my eyes or by a letter. I would hold this picture until it came to me spontaneously and naturally—until when I prayed for the person who had been ill I would see him well instantly, not by an act of will but by the joyful and triumphant belief that it was so. And feeling this joy and this power, I would dare to say, "Amen: So be it." When we are really infused with the power of God it is our natural impulse to speak thus with authority. God created with the word of power. He said, "Let there be light," and there was light. Jesus, the love-manifestation of God, healed with the word of power. His healings sprang from that continual communion with God that He found through prayer upon the mountain-tops. "The Father that dwelleth in me doeth the works," He said. But His healings were projected by the word of power, and the only spoken part of the foundation-prayer on which His works rested was the word of command: "Arise and walk!" "I say unto thee, arise!"

As He fills us with Himself there comes to us more and more the inner sense of His authority, so that we dare to say in His name, "I direct and command the forces of the body to throw off this disease and be well! Let it be so! Amen!"

And the spirit within us knows when that word shall accomplish the thing whereto we send it, and shall not return unto us void. For as we send forth the word of power, we sink deep into the humanity of those for whom we pray, seeing them perfect through the eyes of human understanding and love, and listening as it were, for the return messages of their spirit into ours. More and more we know by our own feelings whether our prayers have reached them or whether they have not.

Therefore, having constructed by thought and will a picture of the patient well, peaceful and happy, we then ask Jesus Himself to go through us and abide in the one for whom we pray, resurrecting him after that likeness of all beauty that is Himself. And believing that He is doing so, we learn to see within the patient, Christ.

If we meditate too much upon our own power as children of God, we tend to become conceited and remote from men. But no danger can befall us when we meditate upon the power of Jesus Christ and the wonderful love with which He gives that power to us. The man Jesus has already accomplished for us that most mysterious of all miracles, the stepping-down of the high voltage of God's creativity to a wave-length that our little beings can endure. We cannot look upon God and live. Too much dwelling on His impersonal light shrivels our personalities by burning out that very humanity that He came to save. But as we receive life through the Life-Giver, we receive a voltage of heavenly electricity that enriches our human personalities and deepens our human love. We find that as we learn to see Him in all men, we love all people more and more. We love them not in some mystic, esoteric "spiritual plane," but just as friends. Only as human friends can we help them, for only through our humanity can God reach the humanity of others. As Thomas Kelly says, "First He takes the world out of our hearts, so that we can give our hearts to Him. Then He puts the world back into our hearts, so that we can give Him to the world."

This then is the triple process for which we are called: reaching the white light of the creator God, finding the human loveliness of Jesus Christ, and by the power of the Holy Spirit recreating man in the image of Christ through seeing Christ in man.

This is, indeed, Christianity. Every other way of thought

finds God by leaving man. In Jesus alone the Word was made flesh and dwelt among us.

As we abide in Him, we do not deny but fulfill every possibility of our humanity. We manifest the glory of God, not by setting aside personal love that the impersonal may flow in, but by learning to feel personal love toward everyone and everything. He loved every man and woman and child, every bird of the air and every lily of the field, all beautiful and lovely things that God has made. And as we rise into the divinity of God through the humanity of Jesus, we find that we too love more and more all beautiful and lovely things that God has made. We hear in music the undertones and overtones of heaven. We see in flowers a depth and richness and poignancy that we had never seen before. Our hearts beat with the world's heart in an almost unbearable sympathy that is full of joy, for we see the joy that is about to burst upon the world. Our children fill us with a deep and tender glow of love and of delight. And the love of wife and husband flows more fully and happily in every normal channel that God made for its release.

Then if we would help man through intercession, we must hold God by one hand and man by the other hand, never separating ourselves either from the love of God or from the love of man. As we do this by the indwelling of Jesus Christ, God can work through our normal human love in ways that we do not see. He will use it to the fullest, divesting its main flow often from those who first aroused our love to those who most need His love. Because we love His little ones in a simple human way, a way that they can understand, because we so love them in all their weakness and stupidity and suffering, they love us. And because they love us, they feel the healing love of the Father shining through the human love of little hearts. Thus our simple human love will be used for divine purposes. And as it is so used, it will become more unselfish, more universal, more real and deep and vital until one day it is indeed filled with all the fullness of God.

As Hosea said, we draw them "with cords of a man, with bands of love."

14

Two Or Three Gathered Together

"Where two or three are gathered together in My name," Jesus said, "there am I, in the midst." And He said in the preceding verse that if even two of them agreed on a prayer request it would be done for them by His Father. He offered no explanation of this special authority in prayer given to two or three praying together. He merely stated it because it is true. He discovered through His own prayer-work the value of cooperation. When he raised Jairus' daughter from the dead, He took with Him Peter, James and John. He sought the cooperation of the same three when He undertook that most awful and mysterious work of prayer that we call the Redemption: that work of receiving into Himself the spirits of all men, purging them of their sins through His own suffering and re-charging them with the love of God. The three who helped Him in this work were overcome with exhaustion; they slept. Yet He used even the tiny bit of help that they could give Him, for He needed them.

He uses every little bit of help that we can give Him today, for He needs us. And where two or three are gathered together in His name, their combined thought-vibrations make a wider channel for the inflow and out-flow of His love. Knowing the power that could thus be set free He said that they might ask what they would, and it would be done unto them.

The method of a small group thus gathered together in prayer can be as free as the wind, as free as the air, for on entering the world of prayer we enter into the glorious liberty of the sons of God. We make in silence our prepara-tion of forgiveness and peace and reach out for the light of God and the indwelling of Jesus Christ. Having made this preparation we continue to sit in silence, waiting for the guidance of the Holy Spirit. As He gives His children one by one into our minds so that we can love them back to health and happiness, we mention them aloud. Sometimes we mention only the name, and see within our minds the perfection that is God's will for this His child. Sometimes we state aloud in precise words that definite working of God's spirit that we feel to be His will for this His child. Sometimes we feel impelled to send forth by a rush of outgoing faith the word of healing saying as He said, "Be healed!" "Arise and walk!"

One cannot force this work of healing. But when it comes spontaneously, we may be assured that our prayers have availed.

One evening six or seven of us were to meet for prayer in the chapel. One of our group happened to be in Baltimore, at the bedside of a nephew dangerously ill. The young man had been infected by a burst appendix and now suffered from peritonitis, an infected kidney and a streptococcic infection of the blood stream. The aunt, a trained nurse, thoroughly understood the danger of his condition. There-fore she called up from Baltimore and asked us to pray for him.

"We'll pray for him at nine-thirty exactly," I told her. "Be with him in silence at that time, with your hands on him. But don't try to do anything for him yourself. Think of yourself as only a hollow tube through whom life is pouring, and think of the boy as receiving a transfusion of spiritual life.''

Two days later she returned to our town and found me pulling up weeds in the back yard.

''It was the most wonderful thing I ever saw,'' she said. ''I kept my hands on him for a while, and at a quarter to ten he said, 'Aunt Lucy, what's happening to me? All of a sudden I feel fine. I don't hurt any more or anything.' ''

The hospital in perplexity kept him one more day, during which every test was negative. On the following day, being perfectly well, he dressed and went home.

This incident is upon the hospital records and can be examined by anyone who cares to investigate it. ''It's a miracle,'' the doctors said. ''It cannot be explained by medical science.''

Doctors often make such a remark. But amazingly, for we have always considered them seekers after truth, most of them make no attempt to understand this miracle. If they would only seek its explanation, how tremendously they could increase their own power to heal!

In the case of this boy, conditions both for sending and for receiving were perfect, so the healing was instantaneous and complete. Unfortunately, it is not always so. The current of life is often interrupted by the static of contrary thinking, either at the receiving or at the giving end. For the one who would send forth health must think health and nothing else. If he would inquire of the patient's symptoms let him do so at some other time, and not turn the hour of prayer into a gossip circle. If he would advance his opinions concerning the patient's spiritual condition, again let him do it at some other time. It is not his business to analyze the reasons for the patient's slowness in recovering. That is between the patient and his God. It is only his business to extend to the patient the healing of God's spirit through Jesus Christ, and the Spirit can do His own talking in the spirit of the patient. Many groups who meet for prayer turn into discussion groups instead, and so weaken their prayer-power and make themselves unpopular. For the discussion will some day get back to the patient, who may not like to find that the prayer group considered him self-centered and lacking in spiritual understanding. As for the patient's negative thought-habits, they do not in any way concern the ones who pray. The amateur prayer-psychiatrist is apt to become what is popularly termed "a pain in the neck." He is apt to become inquisitive, officious and self-satisfied, none of which states of mind are states of prayer.

"I determined," said St. Paul, "not to know anything among you save Jesus Christ, and Him crucified."

An excellent rule. If we can see Christ, and Him self-given for the patient, and then see the patient well, healed by the love of Christ, we will be sending forth a pure stream of that love, unadulterated by gossip, criticism, or the consideration of symptoms.

Functional diseases are usually instantly healed if the prayer connects with the patient at all. Sometimes it does not so connect. Our guidance is not infallible. Indeed there is no prayer-work so difficult as the securing of a clear and definite guidance! And sometimes we have tried to enter a spiritual door that is closed, or to take on a case too difficult for our present spiritual development. If we can see the patient face to face, we can find the reason for the failure and help the patient to overcome it. If we cannot see the patient, we must not fret or blame ourselves unduly if our prayers fail to reach him. We must pray in quietness for the increase of our own faith and of our own understanding, and leave the patient in God's hands.

Organic diseases such as cancer and arthritis, are naturally much more difficult than functional diseases. Nevertheless they are sometimes healed. We were once asked to pray for a man of seventy-two suffering from cancer of the throat. The condition gradually disappeared, to the complete amazement of the French specialist, who, more honest than many doctors, confounded himself with cries of, "Extraordinaire! Extraordinaire!"

The patient, being old and full of years, eventually passed away, but of some other malady. The cancer of the throat never returned.

This patient recovered. Yet it is only honest to say that many who suffer from organic diseases are not healed through prayer. Must we then accept limitation in prayer? Must we admit that some things are impossible to God?

Nothing is impossible to God. But some things are impossible to us, at our present stage of spiritual development. We do not accept any limitation in our spiritual growth. We expect to be changed from glory to glory, until we have attained the full measure of the stature of Christ. But we expect to walk this high and holy way step by step, knowing that as we rise higher in faith He will work through us more and more powerfully, being willing in the meantime to demonstrate power according to the measure of our faith and of our understanding.

Doctors believe that there is a cure for cancer, only they have not found it. If we attempt something too hard for us we must believe that there is a prayer-approach for the solving of the problem, only we have not found it. And we must believe that some day, as we patiently walk the road to heaven, we will find it. In the meantime, we will be wise to try the smaller and humbler things, and to refrain from assuming burdens greater than our spiritual strength can bear. We would also be wise not to rush into the organizing of a prayer group, for prayers cannot be organized. They must *grow*.

"How do you start a prayer group?" people often ask me.

I know no way of starting a prayer group except to make my own prayers so powerful that a group naturally grows up around me. This group will consist, at first at least, of those whom I have helped in prayer. They will become too numerous for me to reach singly, and they will desire to keep some hold on a prayer-channel that they have found effective. They will suggest therefore, that several of us meet together now and then to study the things of God and to pray. Thus the seed of effective prayer will bring forth the fruit of a prayer group. For Christianity is an organism, not an organization. It is a living, growing thing, however inconspicuous, like a grain of mustard seed—like yeast—as the One who knew informed us long ago.

The planting of the seed of faith is the first step in the forming of a prayer group. If we take this step, the second will grow out of it. Many people try to take the second step who would not dream of taking the first.

"Wouldn't it be wonderful to get together and organize a prayer group?" cries a brisk, energetic lady, and she accordingly names a day and an hour and plunges into intercessions.

Her group dies out, she knows not why. It does not occur to her that her prayer-partners look at her digestive tablets and her church quarrels, and find no impetus to faith in her example. Nor does it occur to her that she has bound no one to her with the bonds of effective prayer.

I once suggested to a well-meaning lady, determined to organize a prayer group, that she might go to see so-and-so who was in trouble and pray with her.

"Oh, but I can't!" cried the organizer, dismayed. "I don't know how to talk to people like that. And anyway, her house is so dirty it makes me sick."

So she went on organizing. Her services of prayer faded

away, for no one came to them. She decided therefore that after all it was more practical to raise money for social service, as indeed in her case it was. People did not want prayers, she said.

In that she was mistaken. The world is starving to death for lack of prayers, and the world knows it. The world in its crying need makes pitiful tracks to the door of any mystic or seer who exerts a dubious power in prayer, so great is its longing for the actual dynamic of God's love. The trouble with the organizer was that she was trying to take the second step—intercession—before she had sufficient faith to take the first step of direct and personal prayer.

When a prayer group has been formed by the natural cleaving together of those who have helped each other through faith, it will inevitably be a healing group, for nine-tenths of the requests that come to it will be for the healing of the body—the postponing of death. Christians do not like death. They are less willing to die than are many heathen, and in this they are right. For Christ came to bring life, not death.

The prayer group will also need to learn how to send to a distance the protecting power of God. Our own group learned this during the war. Most of us were mothers, and every mother longs to protect her young. Yet this instinctive longing arouses many questions in the minds of those who pray.

"Isn't it selfish to want my son to live while other mothers' sons must die?" some people ask.

No mother would refuse to feed her child because she could not at the moment feed every hungry child on earth. It is doubtful whether her gifts to other children would be acceptable in God's sight if she were so lazy as to refuse to feed her own.

We can protect our sons even in war by projecting love

into the midst of hate. A practical, concise and definite way of doing this is to encircle those in danger by God's love-power. To limit one's prayers for those in danger by the pious ejaculation, "Thy will be done," is merely to evade the responsibility. We can cause His will to be done concerning our own loved ones, if we are willing to make the tremendous effort of being the conductors of love into the midst of hate. Therefore, for the sake of the world let us not say, "Thy will be done," and wash our hands of the matter, Pilate-like. Let us ascertain His will *and do it*.

If a loving earthly father desires for his son protection and peace, how much more shall a loving Heavenly Father? If all men and all nations would throw themselves into His arms, He would gladly lead them all into the paths of peace. Since they will not, He cannot. But if any one of His little ones learns to abide under the shadow of the Almighty, he will be kept in peace even in the midst of war.

The reality of the circle of protection in which those who trust Him can walk was known even to men of the Old Testament. "A thousand shall fall at thy side and ten thousand at thy right hand," wrote the Psalmist. "But it shall not come nigh thee." And it didn't! Many of the young men of our parish told of miraculous instances of protection. They felt it. They knew it. "Oh Lord, open his eyes that he may see," prayed Elisha for his fearful manservant. And the Lord showed the manservant pictorially that reality of protection that Elisha had seen with the spiritual eye: he beheld the hills round about Elisha full of chariots of fire and horsemen of fire.

A missionary once taught an ignorant Chinese woman that she was God's child. This new-born child of God stood at the railway station when a bombing raid began. She raised her oil-paper umbrella. "I am God's child, so I can't be hurt!'' she screamed to the crowd. "Whoever gets under my umbrella with me will be safe.''

Four helpless ones crowded under the umbrella with God's child. When the raid was over, only those five stood alive and unharmed amid the shambles. Under the umbrella of the Almighty they had found their refuge until this tyranny was overpast.

A certain missionary traveled alone and unhurt among cannibal tribes. Years later he converted the chief of the tribes.

"I want to ask you something,'' said his convert. "Do you remember your first trip through this country?''

"I do indeed,'' replied the missionary, who had been conscious on that dangerous trip of hostile unseen presences, of following footsteps.

"Who were those two shining ones who walked on either side of you?'' the chieftain asked.

Nor is it given only to a cannibal chieftain to see the guardian angels of the Lord. My father-in-law once walked at night through a lonely wood, followed by a man who hated him. Years later upon his death-bed the man made a confession to the once-hated priest. "I planned to kill you that night,'' he said.

"Why didn't you do it?'' asked my father-in-law.

"How could I, sir,'' asked the man, surprised, "when I saw a strong man walking on either side of you?''

To both of these men the protection of God was made pictorially, in terms of presences and light.

Some of us yearn at times for such a direct manifestation of His surrounding love. But to most of us it is not given. We see nothing, hear nothing, feel nothing. Nevertheless when we connect with God in prayer and ask for protection we have an inner surety, a consciousness of a place of safety in which we dwell even in the midst of danger.

"Mom, you're *not* going to get on the train and go to Washington to lecture," my daughter informed me after the wreck of the Congressional Limited.

"But Baby, if I were on the train it wouldn't be wrecked."

"Now, Mom! After all, there *is* a limit!"

If so, I have not yet found the limit. Since it became less possible to rumble in leisurely fashion across woodlands and prairies in gentle trains, one must often travel in a hermetically sealed capsule shot from shore to shore like a bullet. But I still try to remember to hold up a proposed trip before Him and get His O.K. on it before taking off. I once flew out of Tacoma on a plane that dropped an engine on takeoff and limped precariously back to the airport. When I asked, "Lord, why did you let me get on this plane?" He seemed to reply, quite reasonably, "So that you would pray for it to land safely." So I did, and we did!

Feeling His "O.K.," we can walk in His light wherever we go and be protected. For He is the Father of lights with whom there is no variableness, neither shadow or turning.

A Norfolk reporter who wrote a certain story probably did not know that it concerned the Father of lights. Pilots flying over the ocean at night, he said, saw a circle of light upon the water. It was too dim and flat to be the light of a boat. They decided that it must be a man upon a raft, signaling for help with a flashlight, and they flew down to save him. They found a man clinging to a spar. But he had no light of any sort! Only the Lord was his light and his salvation.

How can one set in motion this protective force and so respond to the prayer-requests of those in danger?

First, let us be still and know that He is God. He is from everlasting to everlasting; He changes not. This little world could be rolled up like a scroll and taken away and still He would be God, with the power within Himself to evolve another world or another universe should He so desire.

Let us know also that He is love, and that He has made us of Himself and for Himself. Because we are given such great dignity as sons of God, we must learn to walk in paths of love and be willing to take upon ourselves the inevitable suffering of giving forth love to all. We cannot desire the love of Christ for ourselves alone while little children of other countries cry alone in the night from pain or hunger.

A mother goes first to the bedside of the child who needs her most, and let us also go in love first to His own beloved brethren, the Jews of all the world; to His brothers and our brothers, in any land where there is suffering and oppression. If we cannot do this, let us not try to pray for the protection of our own, for as yet we are not strong enough in love to do so. Let us pray instead for an increase of the love of Christ in us.

What happens when we send the love of Christ to these His children? I do not know. Somewhere He will find an open door, a hungry heart, an awakened mind that He may enter. We will never see or know the world-result of this our cosmic intercession. But the result to ourselves we will perceive immediately. For it is this very praying for others that makes it possible for us to send His love into the midst of war and pray with power and with authority for the protection of our own. As we pray for *all the world* in His name, we know of a surety that He is God and that His love broods over jungle and desert and the everlasting seas protecting those who rest under the shadow of His wing. Jesus Christ knew what He was talking about when He advised us to pray for our enemies. He was no idealist, He was the world's most uncompromising realist. He knew that when we become so completely immersed in God that we can actually pray for those who hate us and despitefully use us, then His power flows through us so strongly that we can ask what we will and it shall be done unto us. Through praying for His suffering children all over the world we invite Him into ourselves and direct His power through us to the protection of our own.

Most of us are afraid of our guidance, our intuition, our "hunches." We try to close our minds to them, thereby increasing our restlessness and losing the benefit of the heavenly warning that would tell us when and how to pray.

"I have a terrible feeling about Bill!" a friend of mine once told me. "He's in great danger of some sort. I know it!"

One who knew not the omnipresence of God might say, "Now my dear, don't be silly."

But it is not silly to see a bit beyond the fringes of time and space. It is real and purposeful.

"Then let's send help to him right away," I said.

Twenty-four hours later she called me again. "It's all right now," she said. "Whatever it was, the danger has passed."

Six weeks later she heard from her son on the other side of the globe. He had been at death's door with an unusual and violent illness. "The night I got well I dreamed about you, Mom," he wrote her. "I saw you standing beside the bed. You said, 'It's all right now, Bill. You're going to be O.K.' And my fever dropped that very night."

It was the night on which we had prayed for him.

During the Second World War, our parish did not lose one boy, either through illness or in battle.

"But what if you had?" people ask me.

If we had, I would not have said, "God failed me there;" I would have said, "God could not accomplish that through me because I was not a big enough channel."

However, I would not have wasted time and dissipated my prayer-power by blaming myself. I would have said,

"Prayer is never wasted, and if God's love projected through me was not enough to keep the boy in this life, it will certainly go with him in the next."

I would have offered to God my grief at the death of one of His, destroyed by man's wrong choosing of hate and violence, and asked Him to use that grief as an act of repentance for the sins of the world and as a bit of atonement for my share in those sins. Thus by offering my grief to God for His own use, I would have turned it into power.

We know that the grief that comes from war is the result of man's wrong choosing. It cannot be God's will that man should choose to sin rather than to live in love. It cannot be His will that one of His children should be destroyed by infinite hate when He has saved them by infinite love. God is love, and that love is from everlasting to everlasting and does not fail. The light of His love dims off and on in our small, unsteady souls, but the flow of that love is before all worlds and beyond all worlds, and does not change. We must keep this clearly within our minds, for if we once accept death through man's hate as God's will for anyone we lose the power to protect a single one in prayer. For who are we to pray against His will?

"But if everyone could pray for others with such power as to keep them safe in the midst of war, there couldn't be any war!" some people say.

Of course, there couldn't. And that is the *ultimate purpose* of all this intercession: not just to save our own from the world, but to save the world through our own. Each one who learns to protect his own must receive from God and transmit into the world both love and peace. And as these little circles of light increase and merge, they will spread light all over the world. Some day this light will be so universal and so overpowering that the darkness of hate and fear and bloodshed will disappear before it. He is light, and in Him is no darkness at all. When that day comes, nations will beat their swords into plowshares and their spears into pruning-hooks—they will convert their munition plants into factories for the manufacture of farm implements—and nation shall not rise up against nation, neither shall they learn war any more. For the earth will be full of the glory of God as the waters cover the sea.

15

For The Healing Of The World

As we pray for sick people or for those in danger all over the world we find out more and more that we are part of the world. Christ came first to save His own, and then through His own to bring the kingdom of Heaven into the world. We are slow to believe this, because, secretly, in the depths of our being, many of us do not want it. Many of us who call ourselves Christians have an unconfessed feeling that the kingdom of Heaven is not suitable for people of another color and that an English-speaking God wants us to enjoy a high standard of living while other people perish from hunger. But no amount of disapproval on our part will alter the original plan of the Creator. The more we resist the force that works toward His plan, the more relentlessly it pursues us. The fiercer the conflict against His will, the greater the suffering that crashes wave after wave against the shores of eternity.

The world is so ordered that every person in it is inextricably bound up with the welfare of every other person. For we are all one in Christ Jesus.

Our thought-vibrations are not limited by time or space. The sorrow of a nation is the sorrow of the world, for it creates in the air a thought-vibration of sorrow. The agony of a race is the agony of humanity, for it generates a "static" that confuses the love-vibrations of the whole world. It is a silent and inexorable force that follows us through history, and we must either turn and make friends with it or be destroyed by it.

Some nations have willed to dominate others, and some nations have willed to live alone and make money regardless of others. Both of these wills are incompatible with the will of God, who says that we are one in Him. And through our very resistance God has over-ruled us, making the world more and more a unity every day. He has reduced the distance between nations, so that the sea as a barrier shall be no more, as St. John foresaw. He has acquainted our own men with the lives of all men, and made them see, willy-nilly, the common humanity of all. He has literally mingled the blood of all men, by plasma transfused without regard for color or for race. And finally He has used our own scientific genius to confront us once more with the unalterable fact that we are one. For the atomic bomb has forced the blindest of our folk to see that we must have one world or no world.

We must learn then to pray not only for the healing of the sick people here and there, not only for the protection of our men, but also for the healing of a sick world. We know that this is so. We know that the healing of individuals fades into insignificance before this tremendous challenge, for if the world is not healed of its desperate malady, there will soon be no sick people left to heal and no well ones left to pray for them. We know this, and yet we don't do it. We just forget to pray for the world.

Why?

We do not know why. We mean to do it—we want to do it—but we just don't. Or if we do go through the motions of world-prayer, our prayers seem vague and meaningless.

The challenge is too great for our small spirits to meet. We lose our courage as we think of it. Our faith flickers and grows dim before the world's great need of faith.

There are many saints and prophets, true, who pray for the world with power. But we are not saints and prophets. We are only little folks, who yet want to do our best. How then shall we extend our healing prayers to the healing of a sick world?

My own answer to this is to simplify my prayer-objectives; to choose only a few objects for prayer at a time and to make them plain, concise and conrete. Thus I can extend to them the prayer-methods through which I have learned to set free power. So I can feel the inner assurance that my prayers are producing results, and, feeling this, can go forward with faith.

It is true that all the world needs prayer. But if I undertake to pray in detail for every nation in the world, and for capital and labor and trade and commerce and finance, I spread my prayers so thinly that I feel no force in any of them. My faith becomes confused and scattered. Moreover, I cannot help being weighed down by the appalling spectacle of famines and wars, selfishness and greed and confusion and hate. So my mind is filled with the kind of thinking that destroys faith and destroys power. In prayer for the world, as in any other kind of prayer, God works through my faith. He cannot send His power through much speaking or through frantic pleading, but only through faith. The same laws of prayer apply to world-prayer that apply to every other kind of prayer. The law is that in praying we must believe that we are receiving the thing for which we pray. In other words, if we are going to pray effectively for the world or a sick friend or one in danger or anything else, we must believe that the thing for which we pray is at that moment being accomplished.

Our first step in world prayer, then, is to bring down our objective to something concrete enough and simple enough so that we can believe that it is being accomplished while we pray for it. Only God knows what things these may be. So our first step in world prayer is the seeking of guidance. "Lord, for what or for whom shall I pray at this time so as to further the coming of Thy kingdom?"

Very often as we ask this question certain people will come into our minds. For nations are made up of people and prayers for a nation can often be simplified by turning them into prayers for the leaders of that nation.

My own groups choose one nation at a time for a particular prayer-objective. We simplify this objective in every way that we have learned. First we make in our minds a picture of the nation as we would have her be, so that she may best further the establishment of peace. We see an aggressor nation, for example, shrinking back in her borders and sending out into the world little golden arrows of trade and commerce and financial cooperation. We do this in the same way that we see a sick body well, making the picture clear, concrete, vivid and simple. It is a child-like method, this method of happy visioning. But it works, perhaps because we are childish ourselves. Or perhaps because the greatest powers of all are in the end simple, direct and streamlined.

We see this picture in our minds, hold it up into the light of God's love and bless it in the name of Jesus Christ. Then we state with serene faith that it will be so. And we remind ourselves that it must be so, for Jesus Christ directed us to pray for it and He never gave us a false or misleading prayer-objective. "After this manner pray ye . . . Thy kingdom come, Thy will be done, on earth as it is in heaven."

We then narrow down our prayers and point them into the minds of those men most powerful in bringing into being the picture we have seen. One by one we bless these leaders of nations, hold them up into the light of God's love and send the love of Christ into their minds. Through this love of Christ we call forth the potential goodness that is in them because it is in all men. We dwell upon the broken bits of good qualities that they are already demonstrating, such as love of their own people or wisdom or shrewdness or ambition, all of which can be good qualities if rightly used. We bless these qualities and pray that through the love of Christ they may be used and deepened and expanded to become love of all people, ambition for world prosperity, and wisdom and shrewdness in attaining the same. And we pray that the Holy Spirit of God will accomplish this both directly, by overshadowing and entering their minds, and indirectly by sending them good and wise advisers. And we give thanks that this is being done.

Simple as this may seem it is nevertheless a difficult thing for us small praying folks to do. If we had learned the way of it years ago instead of months ago, the history of the world might have been different. Since we have learned it and practiced it even in our small way, the newspapers have pointed out to us the answers to our prayers. Any prayer group that is sufficiently adept, sufficiently earnest and sufficiently self-sacrificial may try this, watch the newspapers and find out its results for themselves.

If this is so, the reader may ask, why does the world not change more rapidly? Why does not nation after nation leap immediately into friendliness and freedom and cooperation?

First, because the "static" of the contrary kind of thinking is so overwhelming. Second, because the above ways of praying are easy to say but very difficult to do, as the one who tries them will soon find out.

Not only does all the world's hate and greed and selfishness and cruelty set up in the air a contrary thought-vibration, but also the negative thoughts and words of the well-meaning but ignorant add to this negative power. Every idle word about "the next war" tends to bring toward us the very thing that we do not want. If we tried to combat all this, we would become exhausted with beating our heads against a stone wall. We had best just ignore it and atone for it.

Atone for it. Here we come to a fact that is bound to force itself into our consciousness as we pray for the world. We will see that we are praying against the obstacle of closed minds. The sick for whom we have prayed have wanted to be well. Those in danger have desired protection. But the leaders of nations for whom we pray do not at the moment want to be unselfish, loving and world-minded. Their minds are therefore closed to the operation of the Holy Spirit. The Bible calls this closing of the mind sin. And the Bible suggests only one remedy for the sins of the people—a repentance done by the one who prays for the one who sins. So the priests of the Old Testament offered sacrifices as a token of their repentance for the sins of the people. So Jesus Christ offered the sacrifice of Himself for the sins of all who accept His self-offering.

There is within the world a love within a love, a power within a power. God's love is everywhere, sparkling like bright sunlight. But the redemptive love of the Man who took upon Himself the sins of the world is a concentrated vibration of that love. It is capable of burning away wickedness, as the concentrated vibration of the sunlight obtained by using a magnifying glass is capable of setting fire to paper placed beneath it. The stream of God's power is everywhere, as water is everywhere in a river. But within that universal stream of power there is a swift current of a greater power, like the main current in the middle of a river. Only this current, the sacrificial love of Jesus Christ, can find its way into a closed door. Only this fire will burn through a hardened heart.

But how can we direct this great flow of life into a closed mind?

By repenting not only of our own sins but of the sins of the world. By doing penance for the sins of the world, or for the sins of that particular world-leader for whom we would pray, and by taking that one to the cross of Christ and there receiving for him forgiveness, healing and life.

My own most effective way of receiving Christ is at the communion service, for I have learned to receive Him through the sacraments of the church as well as through my own meditation. In other words, I have learned to combine the sacramental with the meditative approach. Not everyone needs to use this double method. Not everyone can use it. Not everyone has access in his church to the sacramental method. And not everyone has the open mind and the visioning faculty necessary if one is to use the meditative method. However, I set them both down herein, hoping that some readers will find help from one, some from another, and some from both.

If the reader is willing to try both methods, swinging from one to the other as suggested in chapters 11 and 12, then let him think of himself, not as a separate individual, but as part of the nation and of the world, and the whole matter will become clear to him. He will see that since this is so, the sins of the nation and of the world are to some extent his responsibility. Seeing this, he will recognize that one reason for the dullness and apathy of his world-prayers has been a suppressed sense of guilt. Dare he pray for the destruction of his enemies? Is this really right? Ought he pray for the power of his own country to exploit other countries, keeping their standards of living down so that ours can be kept up? Has he any right to send the love of Christ into a government that is not fulfilling the commands of Christ?

Different prayer-assignments require different kinds of levers. For instance, our approach to world-prayer can be greatly helped by utilizing the "lever" of the sacramental approach. Without this lever, one must push these uneasy wonderings down into the subconscious mind. They stay there and rankle, for our consciences will not let us forget them. So they reduce our power of prayer. The sacramental method permits us to face these sins of the world, to accept our share in them, to seek forgiveness for them and so to set our spirits free.

So let us stand before God as representatives of the nation and consider whether or not our country has been blameless during past wars. As soon as we let down our barriers and consider this question with an open mind we know that she is not blameless. She could have prepared the way for peace and not for war, if she had begun in time. Nations are made up of individuals and the law of love that applies to individuals applies also to nations. The only way to make a sure and lasting peace among individuals is to win their love. This is equally true among nations. And while it would be a costly project, it would not be nearly so costly and so agonizing as war. We won the lasting friendship of China by returning the Boxer Indemnity Fund, to be used for scholarships to our universities. The result of our friendly policy to China was extraordinary. I marveled at it even as a child, for not a coolie on the street but knew our country for a friend and raised his thumb in approbation upon being told my nationality. Then, alas, we threw away this earned friendship by our national self-seeking and stupidity.

It is quite possible that the Pearl Harbor incident would not have taken place if we had showed the same generosity to Japan in our immigration laws and our "protective" tariffs. This is only one instance of a thing that we could have done to show the love of Christ to another nation, and that we did not do. "We have left undone those things that we ought to have done. . . ."

If we measure history by the Sermon on the Mount, we will find such instances on every page.

Our nation then is not guiltless in His sight. Admitting this fact and seeing ourselves as part of the nation and therefore sharers in the nation's guilt, we see the way of repentance. For it is given us to repent not only in our own name but also in the name of the nation. And this act of national repentance has tremendous value. For as repentance for a personal sin opens the way for a person's cleansing and healing, so repentance for a national sin opens the way for the nation's cleansing and healing, as well as for the release of the prayer-power of the one who prays.

And if we want to open the very flood-gates of power, we can repent not only in the name of our nation but also in the name of our enemies. We can use any grief that our enemies have caused us as an act of atonement. For instance, if we have lost a loved one in conflict, we can turn our sorrow into power by repenting in the name of the unknown man who killed that loved one. This is indeed the very thing that Jesus told us to do. He told us to pray for our enemies.

This is very hard. But when we try honestly to do it, His love flows into us and makes it possible. Then we begin to see the length and breadth and depth and to comprehend with all saints what is the love of Christ which passes knowledge. We begin to see also the shallowness of our thinking, the narrowness of our prayer-life, the hardness of our self-centered hearts. And we are so filled with the love of Christ that love overflows in a boundless compassion toward all His children. We are no longer our own, for we are His. And it is given us to be a part of the redemptive process that works in silence through the darkness of this world.

Human beings are continually forced by life and love to carry the burdens of another or to pay for the sins of another. But they do not know how to turn this enforced burden-bearing into a redemptive act, and so there is little power in their service of love. It leads not to victory but only to an endurance contest. By making each involuntary burden-bearing into a voluntary sacrifice and by offering it as reparation for the one who has burdened us, we become part of the main current of love set free through Jesus Christ.

"But I say unto you, Love your enemies, bless them that curse you, do good to them that hate you, and pray for them which despitefully use you and persecute you . . . For if ye love them which love you, what reward have ye?"

Most people think that we pray for our enemies only so that we may be pious and miserable in a holy sort of way. But Jesus did not say this. He said that a by-product of this most difficult of prayers would be our blessedness. We would rejoice and be exceeding glad. He stated moreover that the man who built his house of life upon these words of His, built it upon a rock that could not be shaken by the storms of life.

A nation is made up of people. When enough people in a nation have learned to pray for the nation's forgiveness and for the world's forgiveness, nations will build their policies upon the rock of loving-kindness and wars will be no more.

Jesus loved people so much that He was willing to suffer for them rather than to hurt them. And this divine love projected into us and through us into nations and leaders of nations is the force that will eventually overcome the world.

Forgiveness heals. War is the working out of man's sin—the rash upon the surface of the deep-seated illness of humanity. As we set free the forgiveness of Jesus Christ toward the nation and toward the world, we set free the only power that can really cure the world of war. In other words, the prayer of repentance is the most powerful prayer toward victory and peace. It strikes at the root of the world's illness. If a rash appears upon the skin of a sick child, a wise doctor does not treat for the disappearance of the rash but for the healing of the inner cause of the rash. Prayers for disarmament or for the settling of strikes or for the ceasing of wars and riots and disturbances in the world are only a salve for the rash of the world's sin. They may or may not be effective. At best, they are merely surface cures. Prayers for the forgiveness of the world's sin go deeper. And in praying them we feel that quietness and confidence that is our strength.

When enough of us have offered sacrifices, like the priests of old, in the name of the people for the world's sins, the pent-up current of the redemption of Jesus Christ will rush upon the minds of men and heal the soul-sickness that breaks out in a rash of war.

So we stand continually between the Redeemer and His people, channeling His love to them. So we retain our hold upon both God and man, mediating His love to nations and to men who do not see as yet the way to follow Him. So in these troubled times we are able to help the world by seeing sorrow and the ending of sorrow.

For after looking with clear eyes upon the sins of the world and assuming our share in those sins, we are able to see the ending of strife and the dawning of a day of peace. After our prayer of repentance there comes from God Himself an absolution. It is a feeling of complete confidence in the willingness of God to use us as channels for His forgiveness. As we feel this confidence we know that the redeeming love of Jesus Christ is being set free in our nation and in our world. And knowing this, the vision comes to us and we see the round world safe in the arms of the Father, with trade and commerce, money and natural resources, love and brotherhood flowing freely around and around it.

This suggested method of prayer for the world, then,

consists of two parts: first, simplifying our prayer-objectives, and second, praying for the world in the sacramental way . . . confessing, that is, the sins of our nation and our world, repenting for them and doing penance for them in our own name and in the name of the nation . . . and having done so, seeing by faith the coming of the kingdom of Heaven on this earth.

This double way of praying is not easy. It would be easier to see no sorrow, to look only upon the ideal, to float above life on the magic carpet of spiritual contemplation indifferent to the griefs of the world.

Jesus could no doubt have risen into Heaven on the glory of the transfiguration, escaping all the agony of being part of man. But He did not, because He loved the world. Loving mankind, He was willing to suffer both with them and for them unto the end so that He could endue us with the power of the Holy Spirit. And in so doing, He Himself, the captain of our salvation, was made perfect. He attained unto a resurrection life.

Some such transformation we too can attain. We do not know as yet the fullness of this higher life. But the feeling of it comes to us as we lift our part of the burden of the world's sins and carry it to the foot of the cross and there win forgiveness through us to the world. For as we do so His love enters into us. It is the deep personal and human love of Him who gave His life for us—that tremendous tide of love that we rightly call the passion of our Lord. This inrush of forgiving love cleanses us from the subconscious blood-guiltiness that is our share of the world's sins. It releases our prayer-power. And it affords us now and then a glimpse of a resurrection-life so glorious that we hardly dare to look at it.

"Eye hath not seen, nor ear heard, neither have entered in to the heart of man, the things which God hath prepared for them that love Him."

So as we follow Him all the way, giving of ourselves completely for the love of the world, we are raised with Him into a higher and deeper understanding both of God and of man. We do not rise into the spiritual kingdom and leave the world we love, nor do we sink into the world and leave the heights of spiritual power. In a way so marvelous that only He could have wrought it, we walk sure-footedly in both. We feel the high and holy joys of eternity and also the deep and tender joys of this small earth. We see the glory of the kingdom of Heaven and also the beauty of this intricate round world, enwrapped in the deep sea and folded over tenderly with clouds.

For as we function both as kings and as priests, we walk the way that Jesus walked before us. This is a path worn smooth by millions of praying minds. As we climb this path we tune in to the whole prayer-power of the blessed company of all believers, those in the flesh and those out of the flesh. More and more we become aware, as we walk as children of light, of the tremendous force of this heavenly cooperation. And more and more we become aware of one great helper, one most loving friend, Jesus.

As His radiance fills our lives, we see the world lit once more with the beauty and the wonder of the first creation of God. We feel again the lightsomeness and joy that came unbidden to our childlike hearts. Once more the air is filled with dancing specks of light. Once more the flowers glow with the radiance of eternity and their beauties unfold before us, hue on hue, until we can hardly bear the ache of loving them.

But most beautiful in all the world to our newly comprehending eyes is man, whom God made in His image and likeness and into whom He breathed the breath of Life. Man. Not only the spiritual reality within him but man himself, with all of his tender and enduring human love, all of his pitiable human frailty, all of his warm, endearing

174   *THE HEALING LIGHT*

lust for life. Man, poised between two worlds, bearing in his frail body the glory of eternity. Man, forever failing yet forever destined to succeed. Man, defeated time and again, yet forever destined to triumph through Jesus Christ. Man, dying from generation to generation, yet forever destined to live!

About the Author

Ever since the original publication of *The Healing Light* in 1947, Agnes Sanford has emerged as a leading teacher and practitioner of the healing ministry within the church. Her message is even more timely today, as the gift of healing has gained wide acceptance within the entire Christian community. Her writings have had a great impact on developing the healing ministries of such people as Francis MacNutt and Ruth Carter Stapleton, as well as for her own son John. As an advocate of the reality of God's healing power, in her lifetime she might well have been referred to as "the grandmother of the healing movement."

In addition to the best-selling *The Healing Light*, she has written *The Healing Gifts of the Spirit* and *The Healing Power of the Bible*; a biography, *Sealed Orders*; several novels, among them *Lost Shepherd* and *Route 1*; and two children's books, *Let's Believe* and *Pasture for Peterkin*.